TECHNICAL DRAWING FOR FASHION

LAURENCE KING

Copyright © 2010 Central Saint
Martins College of Art & Design,
University of the Arts, London.
Published in 2010 by Laurence King
Publishing in association with Central
Saint Martins College of Art & Design

This book has been produced by
CENTRAL SAINT MARTINS
BOOK CREATION
Southampton Row, London,
WC1B 4AP, United Kingdom

LAURENCE KING PUBLISHING LTD
361–373 City Road, London,
EC1V 1LR, United Kingdom
T +44 20 7841 6900
F +44 20 7841 6910
enquiries@laurenceking.com
www.laurenceking.com

A catalogue record for this book is available
from the British Library.

ISBN: 978 1 85669 618 0

TEXT BY Basia Szkutnicka

TECHNICAL DRAWINGS BY
Ayako Koyama

DESIGN BY Melanie Mues,
Mues Design, London

TOILES CREATED BY Anne Stafford

SENIOR EDITOR Gaynor Sermon

Author's dedication: to Mimi

Reprinted 2011, 2012, 2013, 2014

Printed in China

TECHNICAL DRAWING FOR FASHION

BASIA SZKUTNICKA

LAURENCE KING PUBLISHING

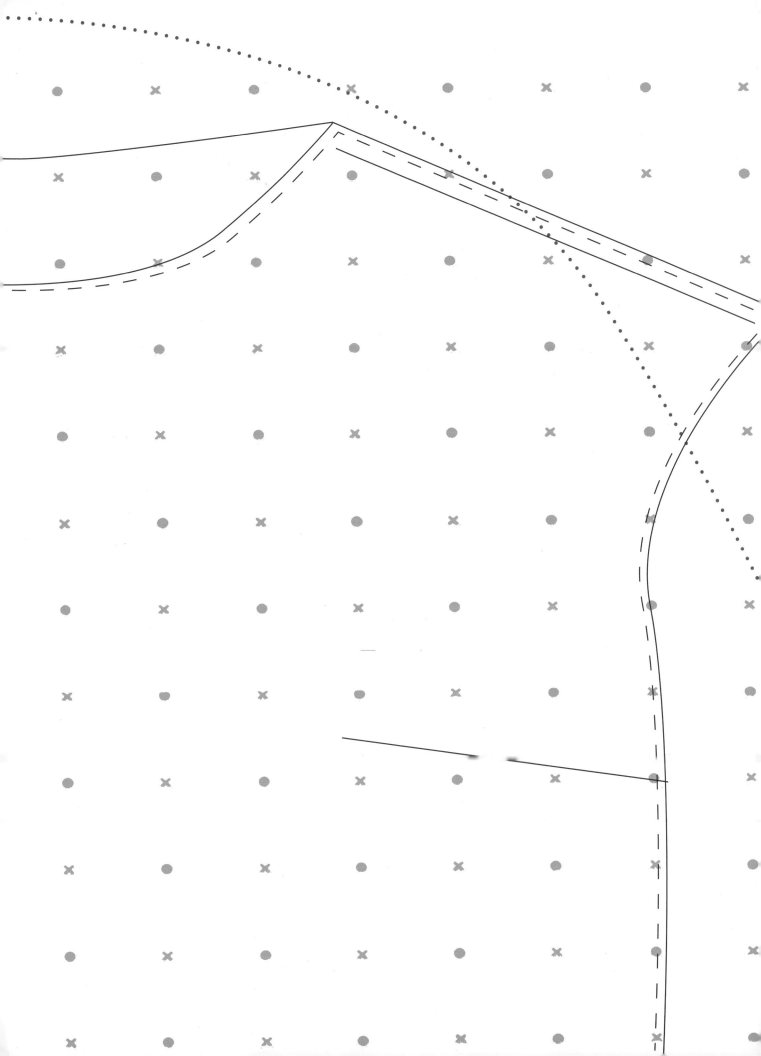

CONTENTS

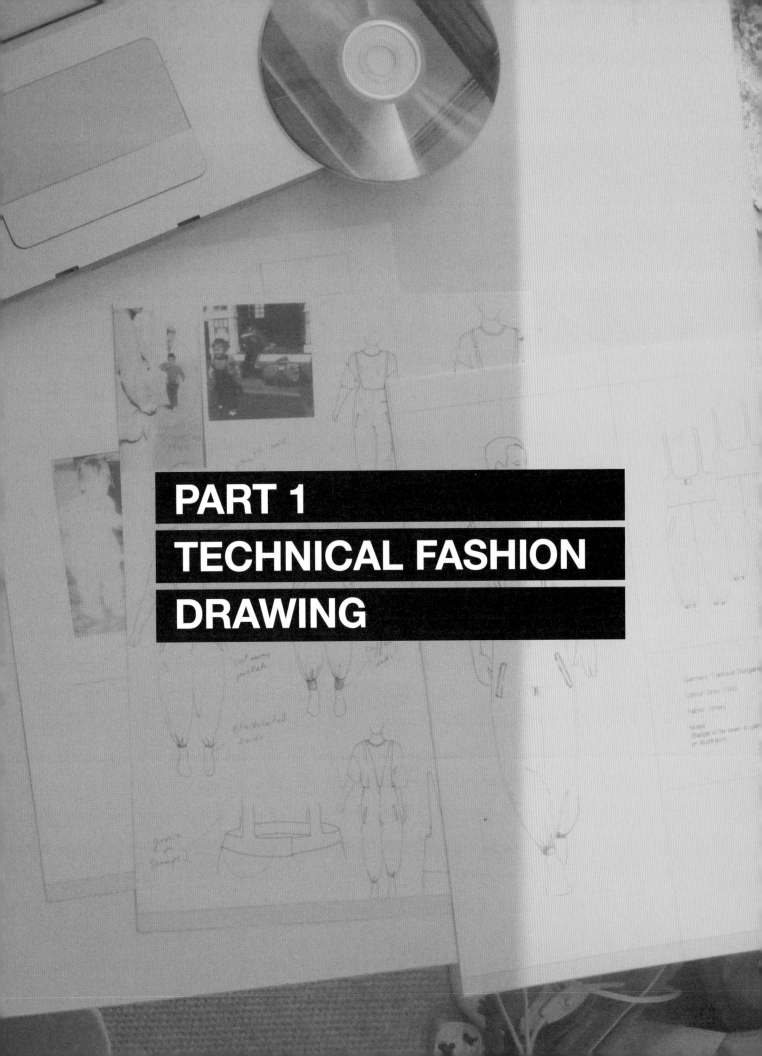

PART 1
TECHNICAL FASHION
DRAWING

Date: 20/8

2cm RIB

Concealed zip pocket.

RIB

78.5cm

Notes: FRONT PANELING MATCHES
that of RIB panel Joggings

Fabric:

INTRODUCTION

The ability to produce technical drawings, or flats, is a necessary skill in the fashion industry. Technical drawings are used to convey a design idea and all its construction details to anyone involved in the production process. They are also an effective way of communicating silhouette, proportion and detail. Differently adapted technical drawings are used on range boards, costing sheets, specification sheets, on paper patterns, in fashion forecasting publications, look books, sales books and catalogues.

With production services being sourced from a host of international locations, any means that can be found to overcome language and skill barriers can provide a very effective way of speeding up the production process and eliminating errors caused by misunderstandings. Drawing offers a universal means of communication, a visual language to facilitate this.

In this book you will learn how to communicate your design ideas using technical drawings. The technique demonstrated starts with the creation of a generic body template, which can then be adapted and used to create the technical drawing. This can be done by hand or using CAD, or a combination of the two. Both hand-drawn and CAD methods are shown in the book, the latter demonstrated using Adobe Illustrator. The aim is to convey basic information and demonstrate a skill, rather than to teach a drawing style. However, no two people's technical drawings will be exactly alike and there is room to develop your own personal style.

The techniques demonstrated in this book will result in a technical drawing that can be used and understood across all branches/sectors/stages of the fashion industry. In addition, the simple step-by-step method can also be used as part of the creative design process. Using a process called 'speed designing' you will see how, once a garment template has been drawn, it can be used as inspiration for an almost limitless range of garment shapes and details.

A fundamental requirement for fashion design is a sound knowledge of the basics: understanding key basic garment styles and their construction will enable you to develop and design endless variations. The second part of the book presents a visual directory of classic garment shapes and their variations, key garment styling and details, as well as the names by which each is most commonly known. By presenting the basic styles as a calico toile photographed on a mannequin as well as in the form of a technical drawing, you will be able to understand how to translate a three-dimensional shape into a two-dimensional, or flat, drawing.

Armed with this basic information, and following the simple step-by-step method, you will be able to create your own templates – or utilize those provided – to produce your own finished garment designs, while developing your own unique style of drawing.

ILLUSTRATION IN THE FASHION PROCESS

Technical drawing is one of the methods used in the fashion design process to present a garment in a visual format. The others are sketching and fashion illustration. Each has a specific function and thus demands a specific set of drawing requirements and techniques.

SKETCHING

A sketch is a rough, spontaneous drawing that is not necessarily accurate or even in proportion. It is the beginning of an idea, the inspiration. You can sketch from your imagination, from an existing style or from reference. If you are producing shop reports, or gathering field information, the aim is to note down a rough interpretation of a garment with key details that can be deciphered easily at a later stage if required.

Part of design development, the sketching process is when you let your imagination run riot, investigating sources of inspiration and abstract themes. It is the stage when you can work freely and experiment, thinking on paper. Usually produced by hand, the sketches can be drawn using any media.

FASHION ILLUSTRATION

The aim of a fashion illustration is to seduce and enhance, rather than provide technical information. Apparel is often illustrated on the figure to give an idea of a garment's proportions and how it will look when worn. Fashion illustrations are used in advertising, in catalogues, magazines, brochures, pattern books and promotional material. A successful illustration will show mood, attitude, silhouette, proportion and colour to assist in the marketing of the garment. Its aim is to sell individual garments or to promote a brand.

Containing emotion, energy, flair, creativity, and often movement, the fashion illustration allows the illustrator artistic freedom to inject their own personality and character into the drawing. With this freedom comes the artistic licence to alter the proportions of the female body. Traditionally, the proportion of the female figure in fashion illustration is measured in heads, where the height of the figure can be calculated by dividing the height of the head into the length of the body. Fashion illustration typically elongates the female form to a proportion of nine to ten heads, resulting in a visually pleasing slender image, in contrast to the true average female height of approximately seven-and-a-half 'heads'.

Fashion illustrations today are created using a wide variety of media, ranging from traditional artistic materials to 2D and even 3D CAD (computer-aided design) software.

TECHNICAL DRAWINGS

Technical drawings are a form of visual communication and instruction between the designer and the manufacturer, between the designer and buyer and between a designer and a lay person. They are widely used throughout the apparel industry, in the design room (for design development and on range boards), in production (on costing and on specification sheets) and in marketing (in look books and on price lists).

Also known as 'flats', 'working drawings' or 'line drawings', technical drawings are an accurate representation of a garment without a figure, summarizing styling details and showing construction, including construction lines, stitching and decorative trims and details. They are drawn to scale, are symmetrical and in perfect proportion. An accurate technical drawing is usually produced once a design has been finalized. Technical drawings may be produced by hand or using CAD software.

Top Stitch

* Top Stitch
on
pockets.

HOW AND WHEN ARE TECHNICAL DRAWINGS USED?

Technical drawings, as we have already seen, have a variety of uses. Both students and designers in industry can use them in design development, when they can be drawn by hand, while CAD comes into its own for drawings destined for range boards and display presentation. Noted on the following pages are their key uses both within a learning environment and in industry.

Technical drawings drawn for presentation sheets, development sheets, range boards and sheets, look books and price lists can be injected with the illustrator's personality. Different pen widths can be used and a variety of line introduced to make them more interesting and aesthetically appealing, though this must be done without compromising on detail.

For specification sheets and costing sheets, however, the drawing needs to be completely accurate and more diagrammatic in character.

PRESENTATION SHEETS AND DESIGN DEVELOPMENT SHEETS (COLLEGE)

At college, technical drawings may be used alongside sketches and illustrations to clarify construction information and to communicate proportion.

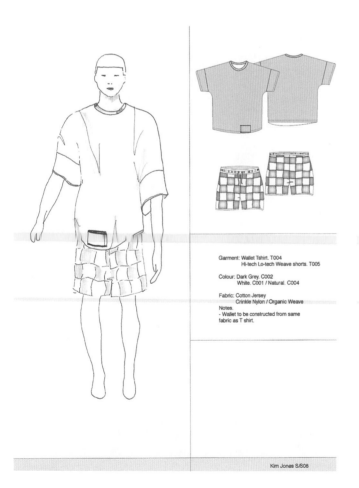

Garment: Wallet Tshirt. T004
    Hi-tech Lo-tech Weave shorts. T005

Colour: Dark Grey. C002
    White. C001 / Natural. C004

Fabric: Cotton Jersey
    Crinkle Nylon / Organic Weave
Notes.
- Wallet to be constructed from same
fabric as T shirt.

Kim Jones S/S06

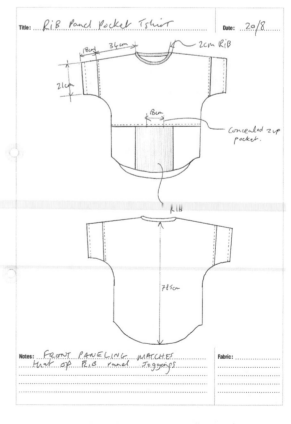

Title: RiB Panel Pocket Tshirt   Date: 20/8

2cm RiB

18cm   34cm

21cm

8cm

Concealed zip pocket.

78.5cm

Notes: FRONT PANELING MATCHES
that of RiB panel Joggings

Fabric:

RANGE BOARDS (COLLEGE AND INDUSTRY)

Technical drawings may be presented on range boards to give an idea of range co-ordination showing individual styles and colourways. Boards produced for industry (below, bottom), and used in presentations, are likely to be much more extensive and detailed than those produced in college (below), but the intention of both is to give an overall picture of a collection of styles or range.

Range boards, with working drawings and style colourways, may also be developed to illustrate delivery 'packs' within a seasonal collection. A delivery pack is the specific combination of merchandise that will be delivered to stores at a particular point in the season, which may represent a key 'look' that is relevant for that point in time.

The flat drawings from a range board can also be used by a catalogue planner or merchandiser to visualize the range in different store classifications, allowing them to determine the size of the buy and to imagine how much of a range will work in store.

RANGE/LINE SHEETS (INDUSTRY)

A range/line sheet is usually produced in industry, rather than in college, and includes miniature technical drawings, often the same drawings as on the spec sheet, showing all the styles in a range. It is presented in tabular form with additional information, such as sales figures, order quantities, delivery period, manufacturing and selling price. An assistant buyer or merchandiser may use this information to update critical paths and delivery dates.

LOOK BOOKS (INDUSTRY)

Look books and price lists may sometimes contain technical drawings alongside a catwalk shot or illustration of a style to show the buyer an accurate interpretation of the garment.

style : 15

price : ....

rt. price : ....

arks :

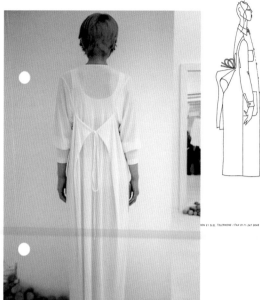

YON £1 5LQ. TELEPHONE / FAX 0171-247 0048

SIZE SPECIFICATION OR 'SPEC' SHEETS (COLLEGE AND INDUSTRY)

A specification sheet, or 'spec' includes a technical drawing (including front and back views and, if necessary, a side view and internal views), plus all detailed measurements required to produce the garment (length, width, spacing, as well as indicators of stitch types, sewing operations, fabric, trims, hardware and special treatments). Enlargements of small details may also be used to highlight important features. These details provide a list of 'instructions'. The sheets are used to ensure accurate fit.

The measurements are either added to the drawing itself, or else included in a table or size chart beside it. The pattern maker must be able to make the pattern using the information provided on the sheet, while the machinist, the maker, or the factory should be able to understand how the style should look in order to make up a sample. Accuracy is therefore vital. If a detail is omitted the sample will not be correct, and valuable time and money will have been wasted.

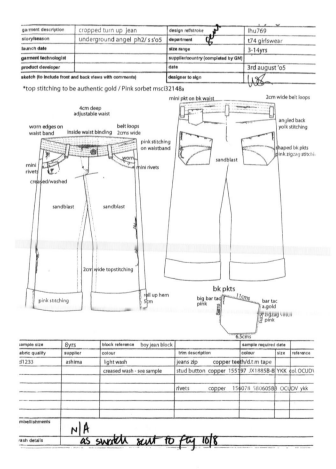

garment description	cropped turn up jean	design ref/stroke		lhu769
story/season	underground angel ph2/ s s'o5	department		t74 girlswear
launch date		size range		3-14yrs
garment technologist		supplier/country (completed by GM)		
product developer		date		3rd august '05
sketch (to include front and back views with comments)		designer to sign		

*top stitching to be authentic gold / Pink sorbet msci32148a

sample size	8yrs	block reference	boy jean block		sample required date		
fabric quality	supplier	colour		trim description		colour	size	reference
d1233	ashima	light wash		jeans zip	copper teeth/d.t.m tape			
		creased wash - see sample		stud button	copper 155197 JX188SB-B YKK col.OCUDV			
				rivets	copper	156078 5B0605B8 OCUDV ykk		
embellishments	N/A						
wash details	as swatch sent to fty 10/8						

COSTING SHEETS (COLLEGE AND INDUSTRY)

A costing sheet lists all the elements needed to make up a garment (fabric, trims, cost of manufacture), which are then used to calculate the manufacturing, gross margin and selling price of a style. Technical drawings or photographs are sometimes added to costing sheets as a visual representation of the garment.

COSTING

Season: XXX			Style Number:	XXXXX	
			Style Name:	Wrap Dress	

Piece Goods	Description	Cost per Metre	Meterage Required		Cost
Fabric 1		11		3	33
Lining		3		2	6
Interfacing					
Other					
			Subtotal		39

Trimmings	Description	Unit Cost	No of Units		Cost
Buttons		1.2		5	1
Zippers		0.2		1	1.2
Threads					
Labels		0.2		2	0.4
Trims 1	'	2.5		3	7.5
Trims 2					
			Subtotal		10.1

Labour				Cost
First Sample	£50 divided across the 10 dresses produced			5
Pattern Cutting	£125 divided across the 10 dresses produced			12.5
Grading	£20 divided across the 10 dresses produced			2
CMT				25
			Subtotal	44.5

Shipping				Cost
Bags/Boxes				0.1
Hangers				
Swingtickets				0.2
Other				
			Subtotal	0.3

Total Cost of Goods Sold	93.9
Wholesale Markup	2.5
Wholesale Price	234.75
Retail Markup	2.7
Recommended Retail Price	633.825

TREND PREDICTION BOOKS (INDUSTRY)

Trend prediction publications may use a particular type of
'enhanced' technical drawing to indicate key shapes and
silhouettes. Artistic licence is often applied here. These drawings
may appear in trend books as well as on a website.

*WGSN (WORTH GLOBAL
STYLE NETWORK) are a
world-leading fashion and style
forecaster. These trend books show
their predictions for two different
seasonal womenswear looks.*

MERCHANDISING PLANS (INDUSTRY)

Visual merchandisers may use technical drawings on merchandising plans to help to plan the display of garments prior to the collection arriving in store. The plan shown here uses 3D visual merchandising software to depict a range of clothing within a store environment. Photographs of finished garments are often used, but here technical drawings have been incorporated so that the layout can be planned right from the start of the design development process. The software even allows for the drawings to be 'folded' for shelf display and fitted on to store dummies.

SEWING PATTERN CATALOGUES AND PATTERN INSTRUCTIONS

Pattern books for domestic dressmaking usually include a full figure illustration accompanied by technical drawings showing front and back views to clarify the style and indicate construction details for the customer. The paper pattern envelope and internal instruction sheet similarly include the technical drawing, to facilitate construction.

The drawings are usually very basic, to ensure clarity and assist the dressmaker in construction. They are often supported by colour drawings of all the pattern pieces, which may include grain lines and other technical details. Side views and enlarged sections (showing details) may also appear here.

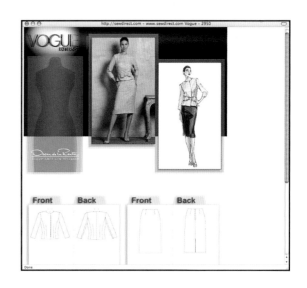

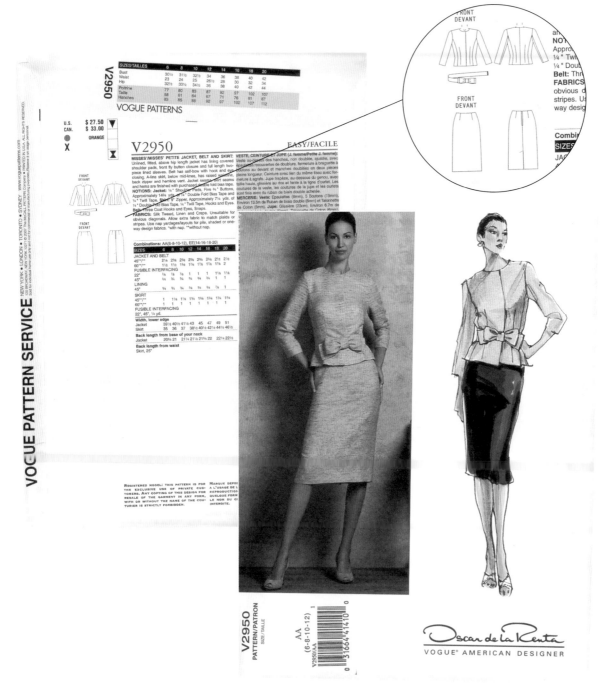

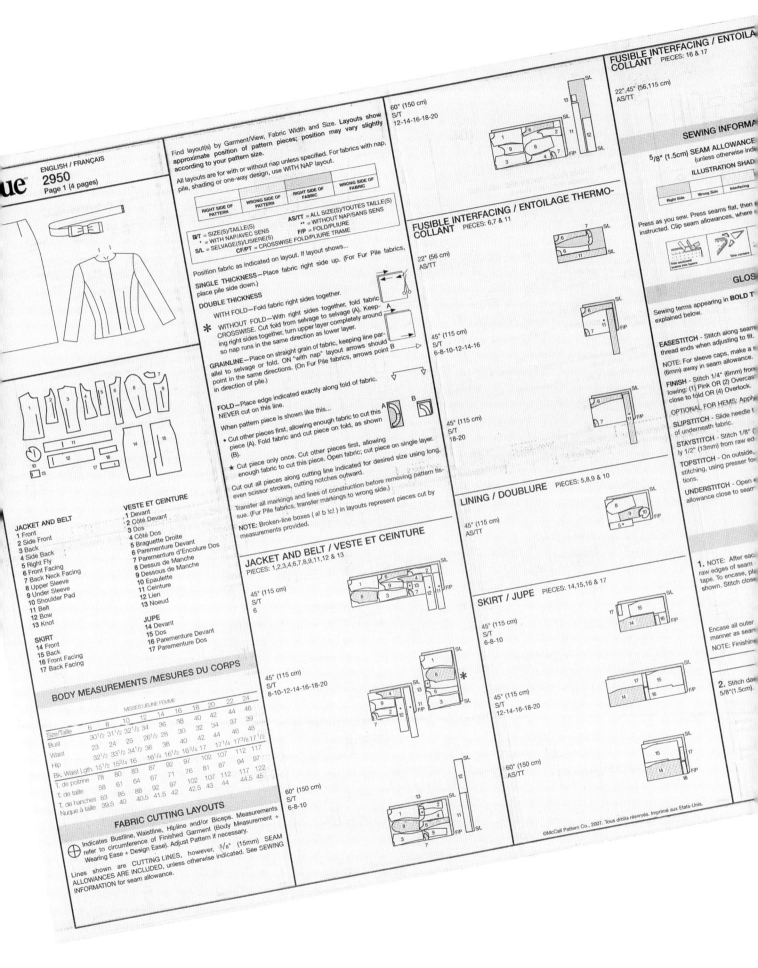

JACKET AND BELT
1 Front
2 Side Front
3 Back
4 Side Back
5 Right Fly
6 Front Facing
7 Back Neck Facing
8 Upper Sleeve
9 Under Sleeve
10 Shoulder Pad
11 Belt
12 Bow
13 Knot

SKIRT
14 Front
15 Back
16 Front Facing
17 Back Facing

VESTE ET CEINTURE
1 Devant
2 Côté Devant
3 Dos
4 Côté Dos
5 Braguette Droite
6 Parementure Devant
7 Parementure d'Encolure Dos
8 Dessus de Manche
9 Dessous de Manche
10 Epaulette
11 Ceinture
12 Lien
13 Noeud

JUPE
14 Devant
15 Dos
16 Parementure Devant
17 Parementure Dos

BODY MEASUREMENTS / MESURES DU CORPS

			MISSIES/JEUNE FEMME						
				16	18	20	22	24
Size/Taille	6	8	10	12	14	16	18	20	22	24
Bust	30½	31½	32½	34	36	38	40	42	44	46
Waist	23	24	25	26½	28	30	32	34	37	39
Hip	32½	33½	34½	36	38	40	42	44	46	48
Bk. Waist Lgth.	15½	15¾	16	16¼	16½	16¾	17	17¼	17⅜	17½
T. de poitrine	78	80	83	87	92	97	102	107	112	117
T. de taille	58	61	64	67	71	76	81	87	94	97
T. de hanches	83	85	88	92	97	102	107	112	117	122
Nuque à taille	39.5	40	40.5	41.5	42	42.5	43	44	44.5	45

FABRIC CUTTING LAYOUTS

⊕ Indicates Bustline, Waistline, Hipline and/or Biceps. Measurements refer to circumference of Finished Garment (Body Measurement + Wearing Ease + Design Ease). Adjust Pattern if necessary.

Lines shown are CUTTING LINES, unless otherwise indicated. See SEWING INFORMATION for seam allowance. ⅝" (15mm) SEAM ALLOWANCES ARE INCLUDED.

Find layout(s) by Garment/View, Fabric Width and Size. Layouts show approximate position of pattern pieces; position may vary slightly according to your pattern size.

All layouts are for with or without nap unless specified. For fabrics with nap, pile, shading or one-way design, use WITH NAP layout.

RIGHT SIDE OF PATTERN	WRONG SIDE OF PATTERN	RIGHT SIDE OF FABRIC	WRONG SIDE OF FABRIC

B/T = SIZE(S)/TAILLE(S)
* = WITH NAP/AVEC SENS
S/L = SELVAGE(S)/LISIERE(S)
AS/TT = ALL SIZE(S)/TOUTES TAILLE(S)
** = WITHOUT NAP/SANS SENS
F/P = FOLD/PLIURE
CF/PT = CROSSWISE FOLD/PLIURE TRAME

Position fabric as indicated on layout. If layout shows...

SINGLE THICKNESS—Place fabric right side up. (For Fur Pile fabrics, place pile side down.)

DOUBLE THICKNESS

WITH FOLD—Fold fabric right sides together, fold fabric CROSSWISE. Cut fold from selvage to selvage (A). Keep-

WITHOUT FOLD—With right sides together, keep-ing right sides together, turn upper layer completely around so nap runs in the same direction as lower layer.

GRAINLINE—Place on straight grain of fabric. Place arrows parallel to selvage or fold. ON "with nap" layout arrows should point in the same directions. (On Fur Pile fabrics, arrows point B in direction of pile.)

FOLD—Place edge indicated exactly along fold of fabric. NEVER cut on this line.

When pattern piece is shown like this...

• Cut other pieces first, allowing enough fabric to cut this piece (A). Fold fabric and cut piece on fold, as shown (B).

★ Cut piece only once. Cut other pieces first, allowing enough fabric to cut this piece. Open fabric; cut piece on single layer.

Cut out all pieces along cutting line indicated for desired size using long, even scissor strokes, cutting notches outward.

Transfer all markings and lines of construction before removing pattern tissue. (For Fur Pile fabrics, transfer markings to wrong side.)

NOTE: Broken-line boxes (a! b !c!) in layouts represent pieces cut by measurements provided.

JACKET AND BELT / VESTE ET CEINTURE
PIECES: 1,2,3,4,6,7,8,9,11,12 & 13

45" (115 cm)
S/T
6

45" (115 cm)
S/T
8-10-12-14-16-18-20

60" (150 cm)
S/T
6-8-10

60" (150 cm)
S/T
12-14-16-18-20

FUSIBLE INTERFACING / ENTOILAGE THERMO-COLLANT
PIECES: 6,7 & 11

22" (56 cm)
AS/TT

45" (115 cm)
S/T
6-8-10-12-14-16

45" (115 cm)
S/T
18-20

LINING / DOUBLURE
PIECES: 5,8,9 & 10

45" (115 cm)
AS/TT

SKIRT / JUPE
PIECES: 14,15,16 & 17

45" (115 cm)
S/T
6-8-10

45" (115 cm)
S/T
12-14-16-18-20

60" (150 cm)
AS/TT

FUSIBLE INTERFACING / ENTOILAGE COLLANT
PIECES: 16 & 17

22",45" (56,115 cm)
AS/TT

SEWING INFORMATION

⅝" (1.5cm) SEAM ALLOWANCE
(unless otherwise indicated)

ILLUSTRATION SHADING

Right Side	Wrong Side	Interfacing

Press as you sew. Press seams flat, then press as instructed. Clip seam allowances, where

Trim enclosed seams into layers.   Trim corners.

GLOSSARY

Sewing terms appearing in **BOLD T** explained below.

EASESTITCH - Stitch along seam thread ends when adjusting to fit.
NOTE: For sleeve caps, make a (6mm) away in seam allowance.

FINISH - Stitch ¼" (6mm) from lowing: (1) Pink OR (2) Overcast close to fold OR (4) Overlock.
OPTIONAL FOR HEMS: Apply

SLIPSTITCH - Slide needle in of underneath fabric.

STAYSTITCH - Stitch ⅛" ly ½" (13mm) from raw end.

TOPSTITCH - On outside, stitching, using presser fo-tions.

UNDERSTITCH - Open allowance close to seam

1. NOTE: After eac raw edges of seam tape. To encase, se shown. Stitch clos

Encase all outer manner as seam
NOTE: Finishing

2. Stitch da ⅝"(1.5cm).

HOW TO MAKE A TECHNICAL FASHION DRAWING

The process of creating a technical fashion drawing, demonstrated here, begins with the creation of a generic body form. This is a basic body shape that can be used as a template, and starting point, for every technical drawing you make. The next steps involve drawing the garment style. Once you have created a garment style, you can either go on to create the finished technical drawing, or use it as inspiration for drawing a range of styles before selecting those that you wish to develop into final technical drawings. This technique of developing designs through flat drawing is called speed designing (see page 29).

CREATING A GENERIC TEMPLATE

As the first stage in the process of technical drawing it is worth taking some time to draw an accurate generic template, or body shape. Once you have perfected this outline, it may be used as a foundation to produce all your technical drawings. Using a head as a unit of measure, the average female figure is, in real life, seven and a half heads high (see right). For the purposes of technical drawing, to create a more visually appealing silhouette, the body is elongated through the lower section into a figure measuring eight heads (near right, opposite page). It is also useful to draw a side view (far right, opposite page) as some garments may benefit from being drawn from this angle.

You can draw your outline by hand or using CAD, or a combination of the two. Since this outline will be used many times, it is worth keeping a master outline in your portfolio for future use or reference. You may find, when working in industry, that you will have different templates for different clients, ranges and markets, depending on their preference. It is important that you bear this in mind when producing work for specific markets.

AVERAGE FEMALE FIGURE

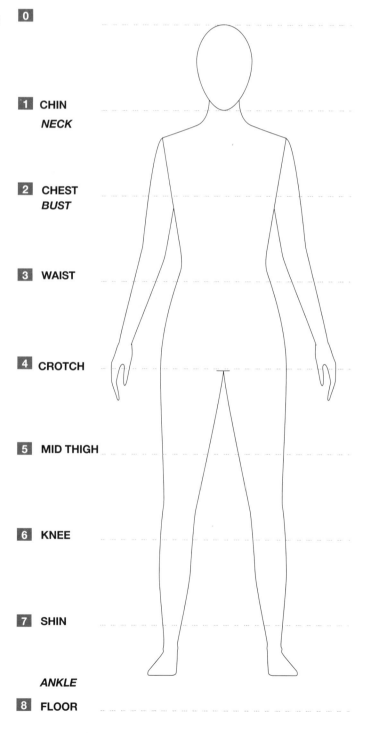

0

1 CHIN
NECK

2 CHEST
BUST

3 WAIST

4 CROTCH

5 MID THIGH

6 KNEE

7 SHIN

ANKLE

8 FLOOR

0

1 CHIN
NECK

2 CHEST
BUST

3 WAIST

4 CROTCH

5 MID THIGH

6 KNEE

7 SHIN

ANKLE
8 FLOOR

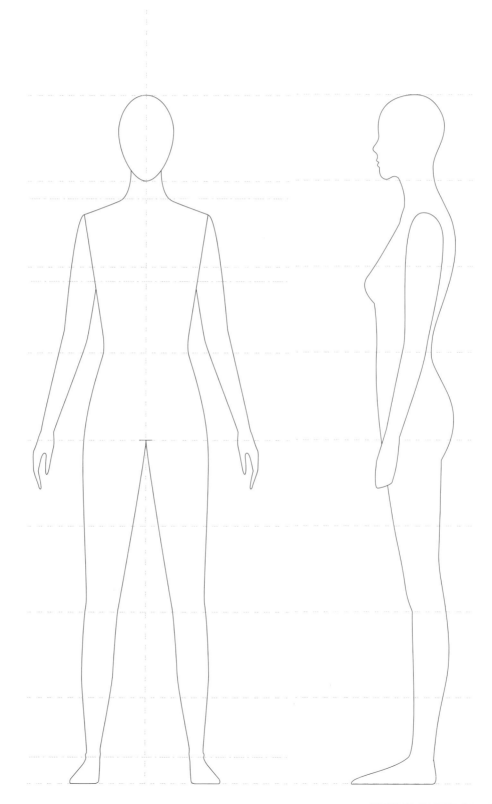

USING A GENERIC TEMPLATE

It is important to understand that one generic template will not be suitable for use at all levels of the industry or in different parts of the world. Body shapes vary from market to market, as well as between different cultures. A female template aimed at the UK or US market might look overweight and too curvaceous to a Far East customer, for example, where the female body shape is different. Garment drawings should reflect the desired market accurately and, therefore, the template needs to be adjusted accordingly each time a different market is attempted. Below is a generic 'western' template. Full-size templates (in proportion with the 'key basic shapes' in section 2) can be found on the enclosed CD-ROM.

GENERIC TEMPLATE

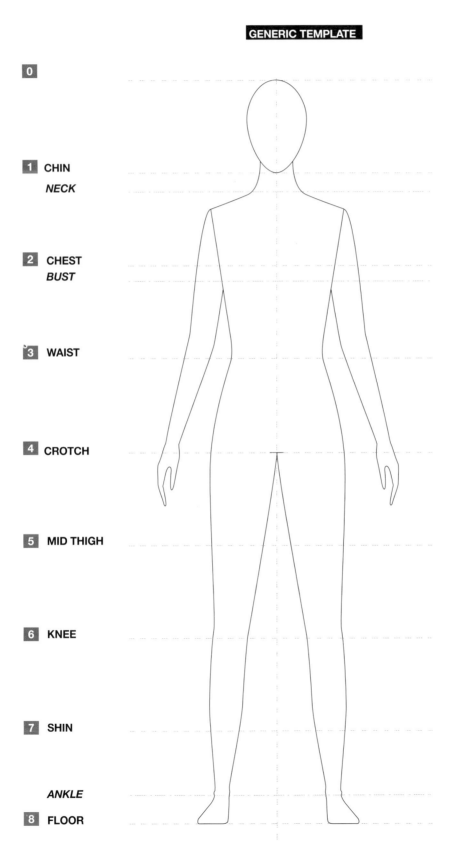

0

1 CHIN
NECK

2 CHEST
BUST

3 WAIST

4 CROTCH

5 MID THIGH

6 KNEE

7 SHIN

ANKLE

8 FLOOR

ADAPTING FOR DIFFERENT MARKETS

The figure, below left, shows how the generic template may be adapted into a 'teenage' template, and below right shows a 'plus size'. The teenage template may also be used for other markets, such as the Asian market, where smaller body frames are indigenous. Knowledge of the differences in markets and body shapes is necessary in order to create aesthetically pleasing templates. If you are designing for a 'plus size' market, you would not use your generic template as it is clearly too narrow. The final drawings should reflect the required outcome as much as possible.

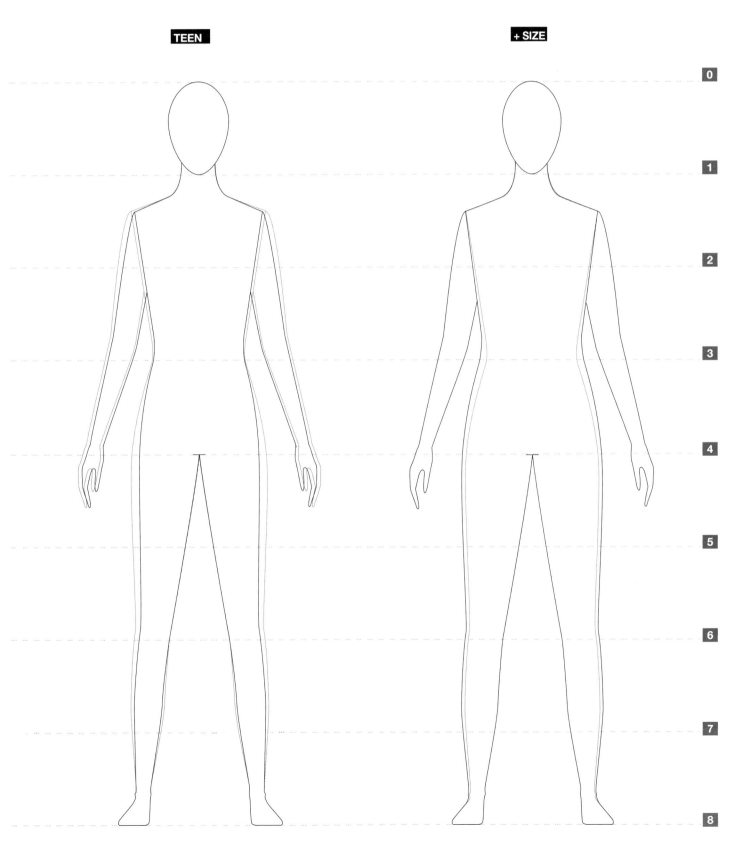

TEEN

+ SIZE

0

1

2

3

4

5

6

7

8

DRAWING FROM A GARMENT

Technical drawings can also be developed from an existing garment. If you are speed designing, you may also be drawing from an existing garment, using it as inspiration or using its basic silhouette as the foundation for your own designs. Using garments from your wardrobe is also the best way to practise your drawing technique, especially if you are unsure where to position styling details.

Begin by laying out the garment on the floor. You should always draw from a 'plan view', from a head-on perspective, therefore you will need to stand directly above the garment. You may need to stand on a chair to view it correctly. Lay the garment down naturally. If you force it into an unnatural position your drawing will be distorted.

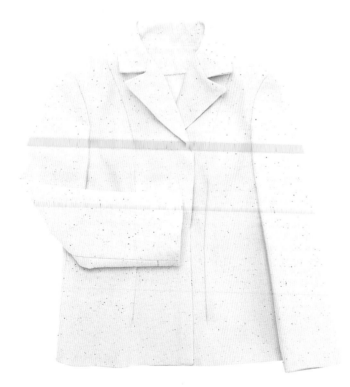

Sometimes a back view of part of a garment is required, such as the back of a sleeve. Working with your garment laid flat allows you to manipulate it in ways that would not be possible were it on a hanger.

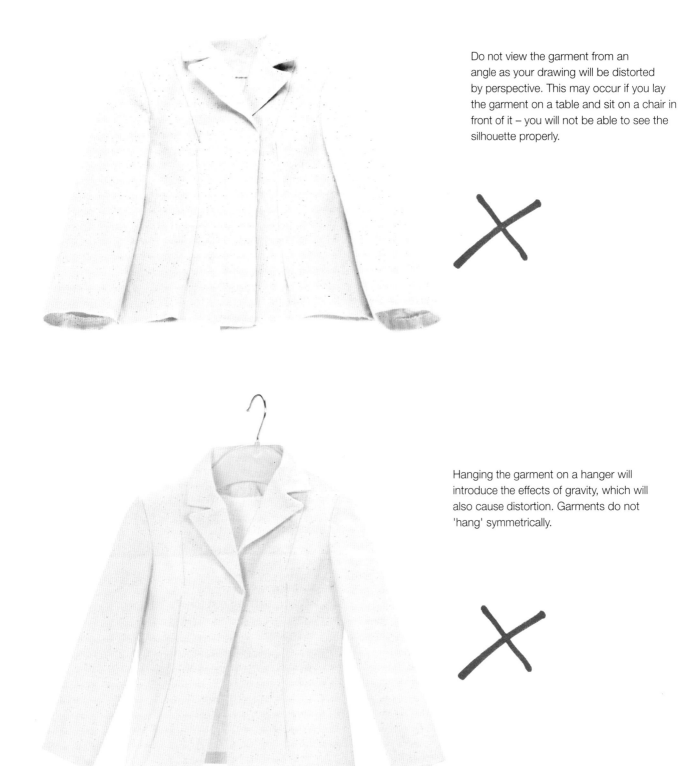

Do not view the garment from an angle as your drawing will be distorted by perspective. This may occur if you lay the garment on a table and sit on a chair in front of it – you will not be able to see the silhouette properly.

Hanging the garment on a hanger will introduce the effects of gravity, which will also cause distortion. Garments do not 'hang' symmetrically.

TECHNICAL DRAWING BY HAND USING THE GENERIC TEMPLATE

Once you have laid out your garment correctly, you are ready to start drawing. This step-by-step sequence shows how to make variations of a flared skirt using the technique of speed designing, and subsequently demonstrates how to complete the technical drawings.

MATERIALS REQUIRED

Tracing paper

Layout paper (45 gsm) or any semi-opaque paper that you can still see through over a light box

Sheets of white paper, A4 or A3 sized

Low-tack adhesive tape to secure your tracing paper over templates

Use of a **photocopier**, to enlarge and reduce drawings in the draft stages

Propelling pencil with HB leads (0.5mm) (Do not use pencils any softer then HB, or the line will not be fine enough)

Black fine liner pens:
• 0.01mm for ultra fine stitch detail
• 0.1mm for stitch and seam detail
• 0.3mm for all main lines except stitch detail
• 0.6mm/0.8mm for outline definition if needed for range boards or presentation purposes (fine-line fibre-tip pens tend to give a sharper line than nylon-tip pens)

15cm flat **ruler**
30cm flat **ruler** (with right angle and parallel guides) or a set square
French curve

Scissors

Scalpel or craft knife with blades

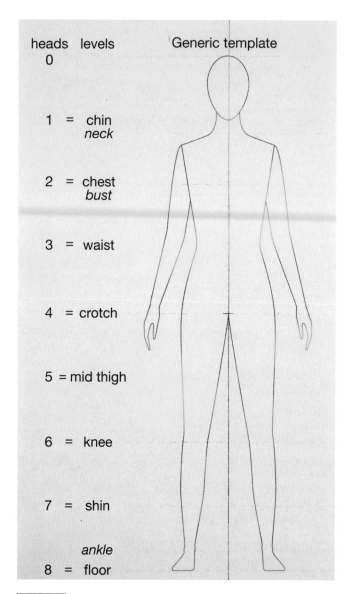

heads	levels	Generic template
0		
1	=	chin / *neck*
2	=	chest / *bust*
3	=	waist
4	=	crotch
5	=	mid thigh
6	=	knee
7	=	shin
		ankle
8	=	floor

STEP 1

Place your template beneath an A4 piece of tracing paper. Adhere the tracing paper to the template with low-tack tape. With a pencil and using a long ruler, draw a vertical line through the centre of the template, and right down the page. You will now draw the left- or right-hand side of the garment only, depending on what feels more natural to you. Draw on one side only. When drawing remember that you are only drawing half the garment.

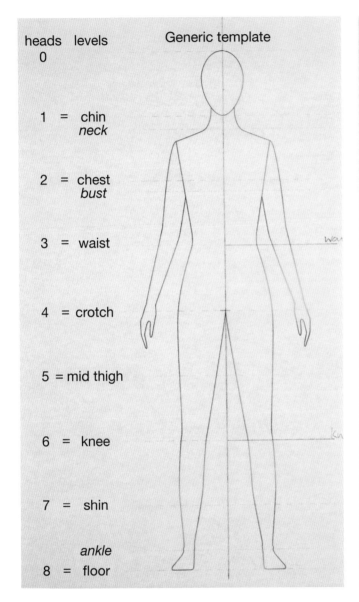

heads	levels	Generic template
0		
1	=	chin *neck*
2	=	chest *bust*
3	=	waist
4	=	crotch
5	=	mid thigh
6	=	knee
7	=	shin
		ankle
8	=	floor

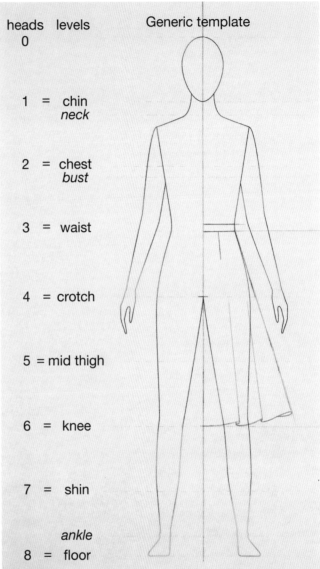

heads	levels	Generic template
0		
1	=	chin *neck*
2	=	chest *bust*
3	=	waist
4	=	crotch
5	=	mid thigh
6	=	knee
7	=	shin
		ankle
8	=	floor

STEP 2

Using your set square, mark the waistline at right angles to the centre line. Mark the position of the kneeline with a set square too. These markers will help you make sure your drawing is in proportion later.

STEP 3

Draw a skirt style on one side of the template. Rotating the paper sometimes makes it easier to 'disconnect' yourself from the idea that you are drawing a garment and allows you to focus on creating smooth and accurate lines. Use a ruler if necessary when straight lines are required, and draw freehand or use a French curve to achieve smooth curves. A ruler with right-angle guidelines will be useful to ensure accuracy.

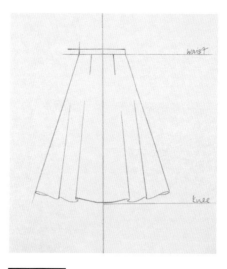

STEP 5

With a white sheet of paper beneath (to enable you to see what you are drawing), trace the lines of the flared skirt through to the other side of the centre line. Be careful when working with pencil on tracing paper, as lines may smudge. This is why you should use an HB or harder lead.

STEP 4

When you have completed your style, remove the template. Fold the tracing paper in half along the vertical centre line, with the side on which you have drawn the half of the skirt on the outside. Make sure you fold the tracing paper as accurately as possible on the centre line when tracing through, or you will find that the final drawing is not symmetrical and will have to start again.

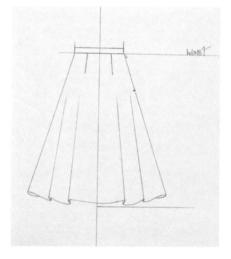

STEP 6

Open out the tracing paper and tidy up your drawing, going over any faint lines. Make sure that any lines crossing the centre-front vertical line are smooth and at right angles. Consider how one would get in and out of the garment; add in openings and fastenings. At this stage you can either complete your technical drawing (follow the written instructions in steps 9–11) or use the technique of speed designing to continue to make variations of the style.

SPEED DESIGNING

Speed designing omits the sketch phase of design work and is particularly useful if you are working on uncomplicated, more commercial design ideas, especially if given specific guidelines by a client who, for example, might commission a range of casual skirts or jackets. Once a garment style has been drawn using the generic template, that style can then be used as a template for developing variations of that garment. Working with your knowledge of construction and pattern cutting, you will be able to draw real working garments, rather than just sketching out rough ideas. Every line you draw will be valid and in the correct position.

All the design development is worked in pencil on tracing paper to create a series of roughs. Each design may inspire another variation; sometimes a simple alteration to a drawing, such as a change in skirt length, waist height or trouser width, will produce a completely new alternative. Small differences between styles will provide more options for selection. Variations can be produced at great speed, accelerated by drawing only half the garment. Each rough may take as little as a couple of minutes to draw, allowing numerous design solutions to be explored.

By working from the generic template, all subsequent styles will be in proportion to each other; an advantage if they are all finally to be positioned together on one page, such as on a range plan. The advantage of working in this way over sketching is speed, allied to drawings that are 'real' clothes. Once you have mastered the basic principles of speed designing, you will be able to develop your own unique way of applying the process to suit your needs.

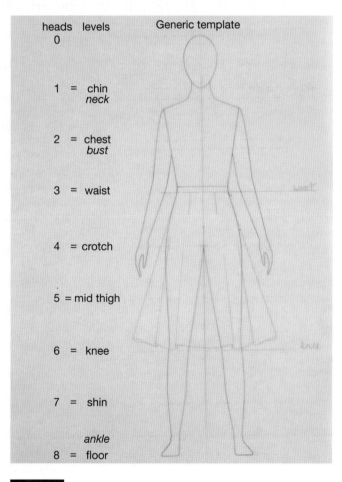

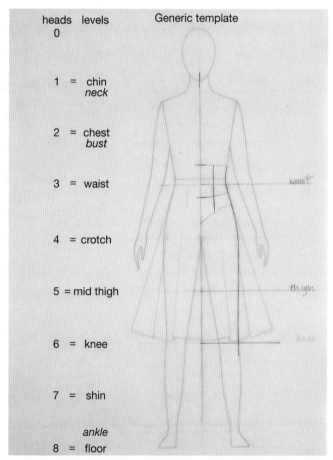

STEP 7

Using the speed designing technique, here we will use this drawing to create another skirt, this time a knee-length style with a high waist. Place the original traced drawing over the template again, then place a new sheet of tracing paper on top. Draw the centre-front line. Make sure all three sheets are secured with low-tack tape.

STEP 8

You can continue to create styles using your original drawing, one style developing into another. There are endless possibilities, and just by changing the length or seam details you can create a new design. In this drawing there are four possible style options: two high waists (different lengths) and two dropped waists (flared and straight).

Once you have a style you want to develop, you may work on a full drawing (not just one side), particularly if the style is complex or asymmetric.

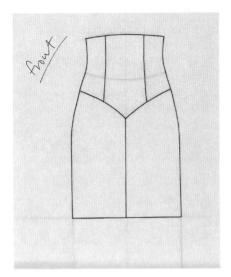

STEP 9

To complete your technical drawing, select one of your designs. You can complete the process by hand or scan the drawing and complete it using CAD (see pages 33–34, steps 7–9). To complete by hand, place your tracing beneath a piece of layout paper and secure it with low-tack tape. You can also work on a light box at this stage, if you have one available, or on a window. You may need to darken the lines of your tracing in order to see it through the layout paper. Test the paper, making sure your pen doesn't 'bleed' on it. Trace over the lines of your design using a 0.3 fine-line fibre-tip pen.

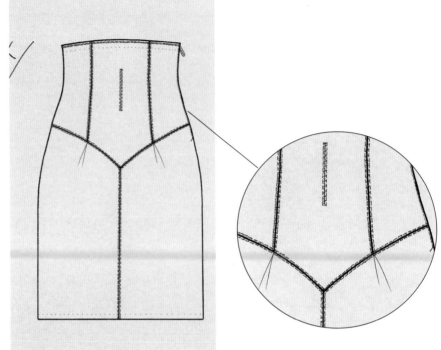

STEP 10

Use a 0.01 fine-line fibre-tip pen to draw in stitches or any fine detailing. If you have a very detailed garment, enlarge your original pencil drawing on a photocopier and draw as large as is comfortable. When the drawing is complete, reduce back down to the required proportions. Remember to note the percentage increase so that you can reduce the drawing back down accurately, otherwise this drawing will be disproportionate to others if featured in a group or on a range board.

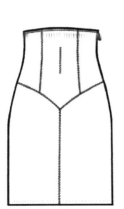

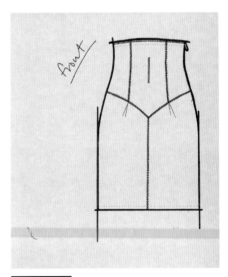

STEP 11

For a particular effect, or if desired, using a 0.8 fine-line fibre-tip pen, draw a heavy black line around the outside lines of your drawing (this would not be used on a spec or costing sheet, only if the drawing is to be used for presentation purposes).

Your technical drawing is now ready to photocopy, scan or use as you wish.

BACK VIEWS

Once you have completed the front view of a garment, you can use it to develop the back view. The external silhouette will be almost identical to that of the front view. Here we will continue with an example of a skirt. Follow the exercise below to see how first one style morphs into another, then how a back view is easily created from a front.

STEP 1

Using a ruler, draw a centre line on a piece of tracing paper. Working from the last straight, high-waisted style, develop a low-waisted A-line skirt in pencil, working in half on tracing paper. Draw lines for both the front and back view at the same time.

STEP 2

Trace off half the silhouette along this centre line. Once you have the entire back view, check for symmetry and make any adjustments.

STEP 3

You may find it useful to use a coloured pencil at this stage so that you can clearly see the lines you are drawing over the template. When working out a back view, make sure any seams from the front joining the side are followed through from the exact same point, unless different. Don't forget to include openings.

DOS & DON'TS

1 If you are drawing a very detailed garment, you may wish to work at A3 size so that you can more easily draw complex details and reduce the size later when you scan it in or reduce it on a photocopier.

2 Never use softer than an HB lead, or your drawing line will not be fine enough for accuracy, and it will smudge.

3 Be prepared to redraw until your rough drawing is how you want it.

4 Always use low-tack adhesive tape to secure tracings to stop the paper moving around.

5 Rotate your drawing throughout the process: it is easier to draw smooth lines when a line is vertical rather than horizontal.

6 Always make sure a line crossing the centre-front or centre-back is at a right angle, for symmetry.

7 Use a ruler where necessary for straight lines, but blend through at a curve to soften. Never draw a curve with a ruler!

8 Never use a fine-line pen on tracing paper as it will not dry and will smudge: only use it on layout paper.

9 Wash hands regularly when working on tracings to avoid smudges.

10 Work in good overhead light so that you can see through the layout paper, or ideally work on a light box.

11 You may have to start a final pen drawing a few times because of wobbly lines: have patience.

12 Always try to work with a sheet of white paper under your work as it will absorb any excess lead when tracing as well as show up a tracing under layout paper better when you are producing a final pen drawing.

13 When working on your final pen drawing, clean the edge of the ruler as often as possible, as the edge collects ink and this may transfer to your drawing.

14 Use a variety of fine-line pens (0.05 and 0.1-0.3) to add depth to your final drawing.

TECHNICAL DRAWING FROM THE GENERIC TEMPLATE USING ILLUSTRATOR

First you need to lay out your garment correctly (see pages 24–25). This step-by-step sequence shows how to make a technical drawing of a jacket using Illustrator and also how to develop different variations with speed designing.

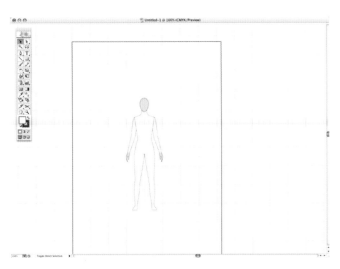

STEP 1
Open a new document in Illustrator.
File > New

STEP 2
Import your generic template and show the grid. Make sure you align the centre-front of your generic template with a vertical line on the grid.
File > Place
View > Show Grid

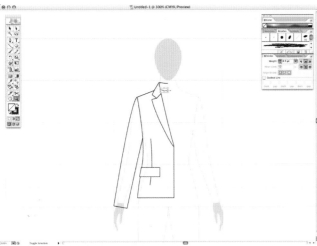

STEP 3
Select and then group all the objects on the generic template together.
Object > Group
Open up the Colour Palette and change the outline of the generic template to a lighter colour using the Stroke setting so that the template acts as a guide, rather than as a distraction. Here, it has been changed to yellow.
Window > Colour
Using the Pen Tool, draw the outline of one half of the jacket. As you are drawing outerwear, the jacket should be drawn outside the generic template (see page 44). The front edge of the jacket can be drawn over the centre-front line to create the necessary overlap.

STEP 4

Always create a balance line at 90° to the centre-front line. This will help when mirroring the drawing in step 5.

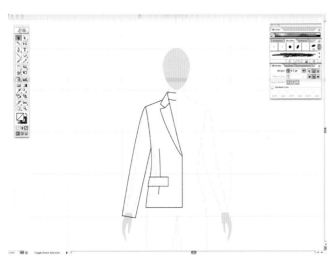

STEP 5

You are now going to create a mirror image of the jacket.
Select and group all the objects in the jacket.
Object > Group
Copy and Paste, then, with the jacket selected, select **Object**
> Transform > Reflect, check Vertical and then click **OK**. Now,
using the Direct Selection Tool, reposition the mirrored half of the
jacket so it aligns across the balance line you created in step 4.

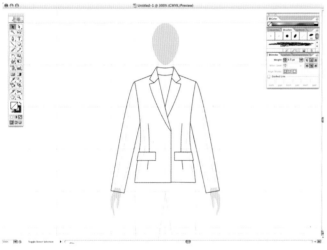

STEP 6

Delete the unwanted overwrap at the front of the jacket. To refine
the technical drawing, raise the underwrap side at the lower edge
of the jacket.

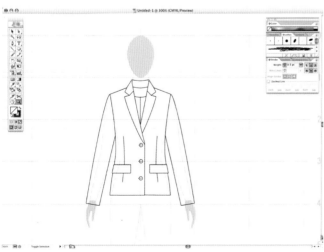

STEP 7

You can now tidy up your drawing. Here, the pocket flaps were
made less deep. The facing and centre-back seam were added.
Buttons were also included in the drawing.

STEP 8

At this stage you can also add top stitching using a dashed 0.25pt line.

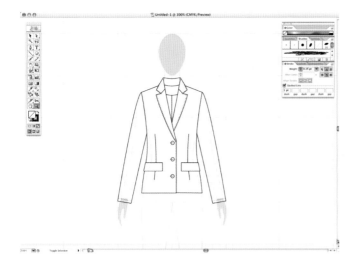

STEP 9

Finally, delete the template and hide the guides.

BACK VIEWS

To create a back view, copy and paste the front view and delete any unnecessary details. For the drawing of a jacket, it was necessary to create the back of the collar, move and extend the darts, extend the centre-back line and level the hem. A vent was also added and the underwrap was raised at the lower edge.

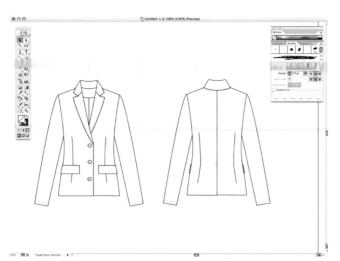

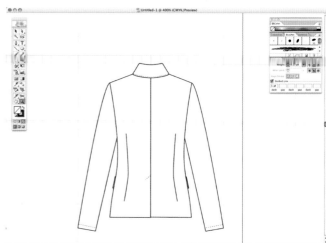

SPEED DESIGNING
USING ILLUSTRATOR

When using Illustrator you can also adopt the technique of speed designing. This can be done at any stage of the drawing process. Using software makes it easy to save and store versions of a design at any stage of the drawing. You can also create your own library of details, such as pockets and items of hardware, to add to your drawings.

STEP 1

Using the drawing of the jacket, first save the front view as a template.

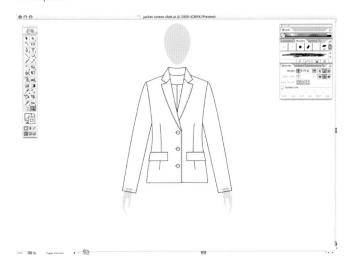

STEP 2

Now amend the style. Here, the original dart was removed and the princess line inserted.

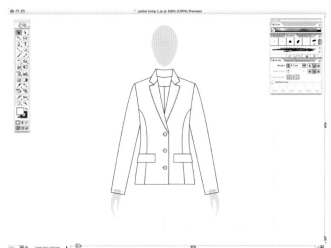

STEP 3

The original flap pockets were then removed and replaced with patch pockets.

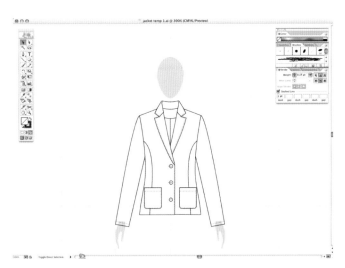

STEP 4

You can still work in half and then mirror the illustration. Here, the line of the jacket has been extended to create a flare.

HINTS AND TIPS

WHAT TO INCLUDE AND WHAT NOT TO INCLUDE

Technical drawings should include only the essential details. If you are drawing from an existing garment, do not draw any wrinkles or flaws in the fabric or construction. Apply a little 'cosmetic surgery' and draw only what is necessary. Look at the technical drawings in the second half of this book to gain an idea of what to include and what not to include.

Below are some basic hints and tips addressing common mistakes often found in technical drawings, using some classic styles as guidelines. Think about the 3D form of the human body and how a garment may need to be cut to fit and be comfortable. An understanding of pattern cutting and garment construction will assist you with information and drawing tips.

Above all, don't imagine or 'make up' how details on the garment should look. If you are unsure about how to draw something, it is best to find an existing garment and draw what you see from that, using existing details as a guide. Don't draw flaws or mistakes.

Avoid overemphasizing details, which might turn the style into something else. Don't be tempted to make your drawing 'prettier' with 'swirly' or 'fancy' lines – leave that for your final fashion illustration.

Finally, avoid the urge to get carried away with your own artistic interpretation. Technical drawings are not the place for self-expression. The purpose behind a technical drawing is to convey information as simply, clearly and accurately as possible. Drawing a skirt as the one above, right, runs the risk of the pattern cutter interpreting this as a wavy hem.

BASIC HINTS AND TIPS FOR DRAWING GARMENTS

If ever you are unsure of how a garment should be drawn, find something similar and check.

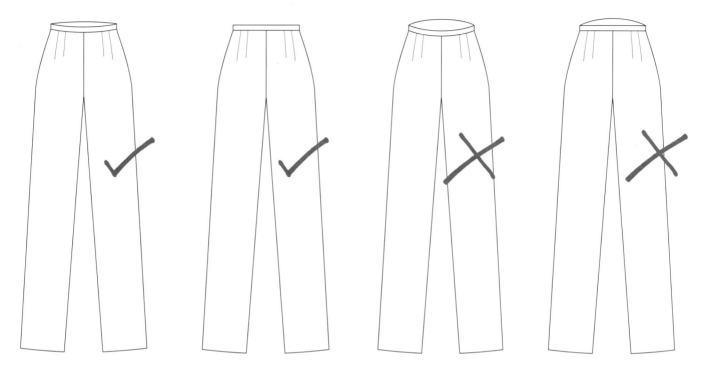

Tops of trousers are usually curved at the top. The back of the trouser waistband is usually visible on a front view, so add it in. However, if the suggested fabric is a stretch material (for example), then it may be drawn straight across. Do not draw overly concave or convex waistbands.

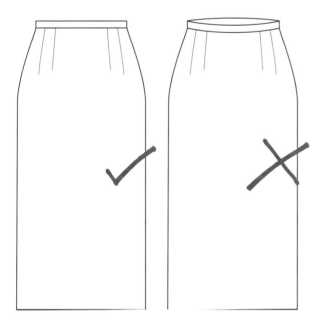

The top of a skirt should usually be drawn straight across, apart from when a style is low waisted – then it would need to be gently curved.

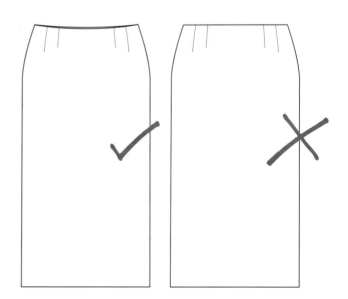

A basic back neck will ALWAYS be curved, to allow for comfort and neck movement. A common mistake is to draw it straight across or concave.

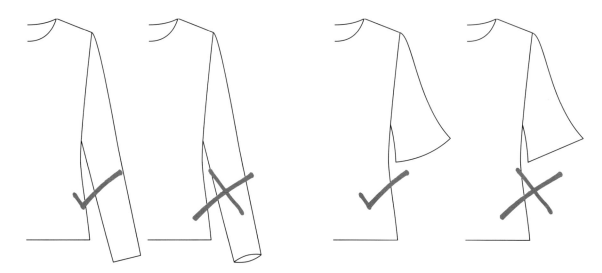

Hems are often drawn curved, but you should only draw a curved hem if that's how you intend it to be. For narrow sleeves (above) and trousers (below), the hem should be drawn straight. For wider styles, curve the hem.

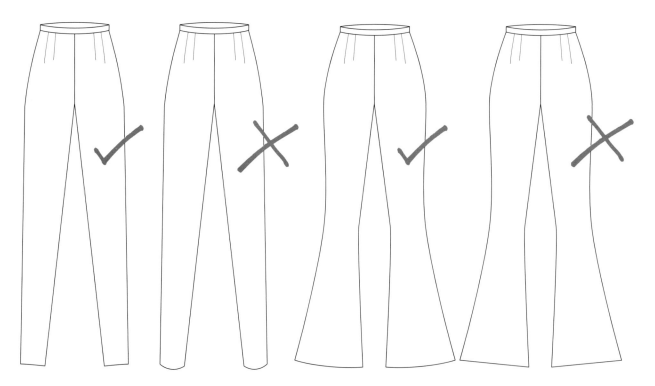

A common mistake is to draw the collar as if it is disconnected from the shoulder seam.

The backs of shirt collars should be gently curved inward: they should never be drawn straight across or exaggeratedly concave or convex.

ALWAYS use one template when working on a body of work, as this will ensure that tops and bottoms will remain in proportion to one another. If you reduce or enlarge a drawing at any time, make a note of the percentage, so that everything can be brought back to the same size. Imagine that all your drawings are to fit the same figure, so they should all be in proportion.

DRAWING STYLING DETAILS

The directory in the second half of this book is offered as a
guide to interpreting 3D garments, styling details and hardware
in 2D form. There are some conventions for indicating difficult
to draw or partially hidden details – such as the crotch area on
trousers or a concealed zip – on technical drawings. Those offered
in this book are one interpretation, but as long as you follow the
basic guidelines for technical drawing, you can develop your
own versions.

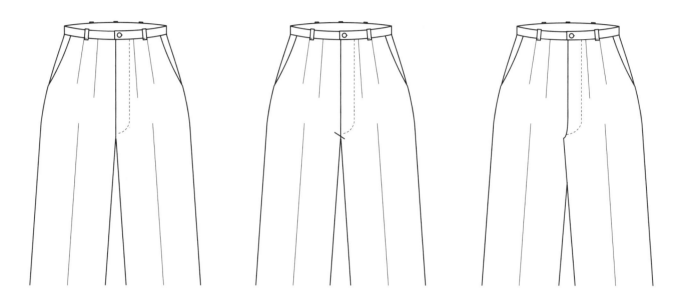

*Though subtly different, these three technical drawings show different but
equally correct ways of drawing the front crotch on a pair of trousers.*

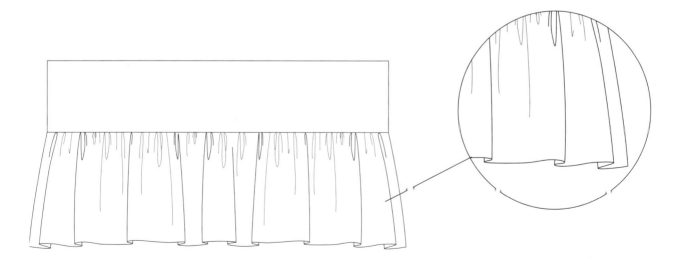

*Flare is often difficult to draw – again, to be accurate, use an existing
garment and lay it out, focusing on the flared hem, and draw what you
see. Give a sense of movement and drape of the fabric.*

There are two ways of drawing gathers. It helps to use a finer line
for these delicate drawings. Depending on the fullness of the gathers,
additional lines (above right) may be added.

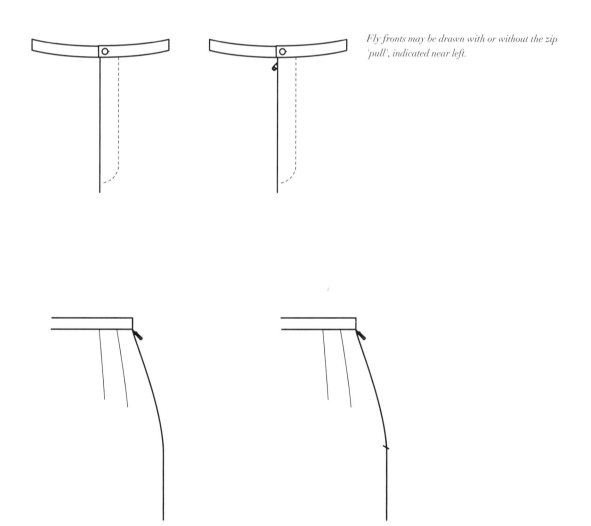

Fly fronts may be drawn with or without the zip
'pull', indicated near left.

Side zips are usually fairly well concealed, so indicate them with a zip 'pull'
and/or a small diagonal stitch. Never draw in the actual teeth of the zip.

DRAWING INTERNAL, DIFFICULT TO SEE AND HIDDEN DETAILS

Sometimes it is necessary to show the interior of a garment, particularly if the specification includes any detailing on the inside, a coloured or fancy lining, or internal stitching, for example.

In these cases you should draw either from the existing garment, or if none exists and you are unsure what to do, find a similar garment, lay it out flat and open the section you wish to see.

An 'open' garment would accompany a front view on a spec sheet, a range board or a design presentation sheet.

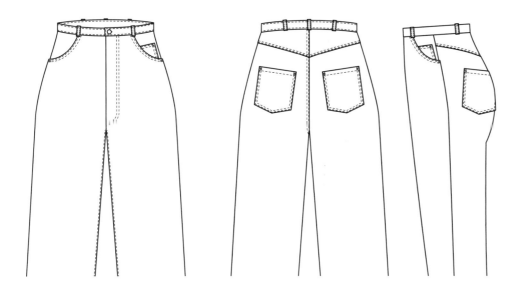

Sometimes detailing travels from front to back over a side seam, or is set in a side seam, so an additional view – such as this side view – may be required.

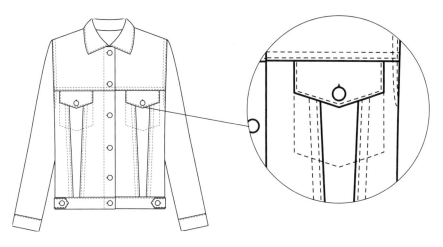

Sometimes tiny details need to be magnified, for example if they are being shown on a spec sheet. Enlarge a required area and show it next to the drawing.

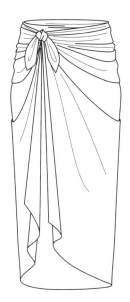

Sometimes you may wish to show a garment unfastened as well as fastened. A sarong, for example, may just be a rectangle of fabric when unfastened and placed flat on the floor, so draw it as such.

Sometimes it is necessary to show information on the back of a sleeve. Draw it as if it is folded back. If you are drawing by hand, photocopy your finished drawing, then cut out the drawing carefully. Fold back the sleeve section and re-draw the placket or detailing, then photocopy the amended drawing and use like an original.

DRAWING OUTERWEAR

When using the generic template to draw a close-fitting style, you should fit the garment to the outline and shape of the template. Outerwear, however, needs to be drawn slightly larger than the outline of the template as, naturally, these garments are worn over other garments. When drawing outerwear, therefore, you need to work outside the generic template.

For ultimate accuracy, if you are working on a coordinating range and need to present all drawings on a range board, you may use the generic template with, for example, a dress, then draw the coat or jacket over this to ensure correct proportions.

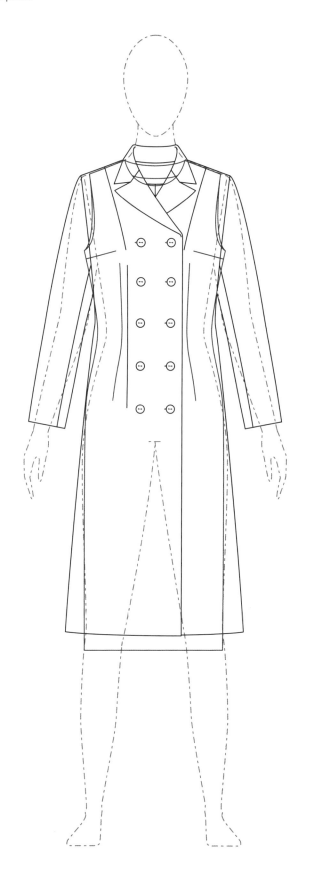

DRAWING VERY DETAILED GARMENTS

If you need to draw a very detailed style and are working by hand, first produce the basic garment with all seams. Enlarge the drawing on a photocopier and, using a fine-line pen, add in top stitching and fine detail. Reduce the drawing on a photocopier once it is complete, and the detailing and stitching will be intricate and accurately represented. You may also want to show enlarged images of particularly detailed or elaborate sections for clarity.

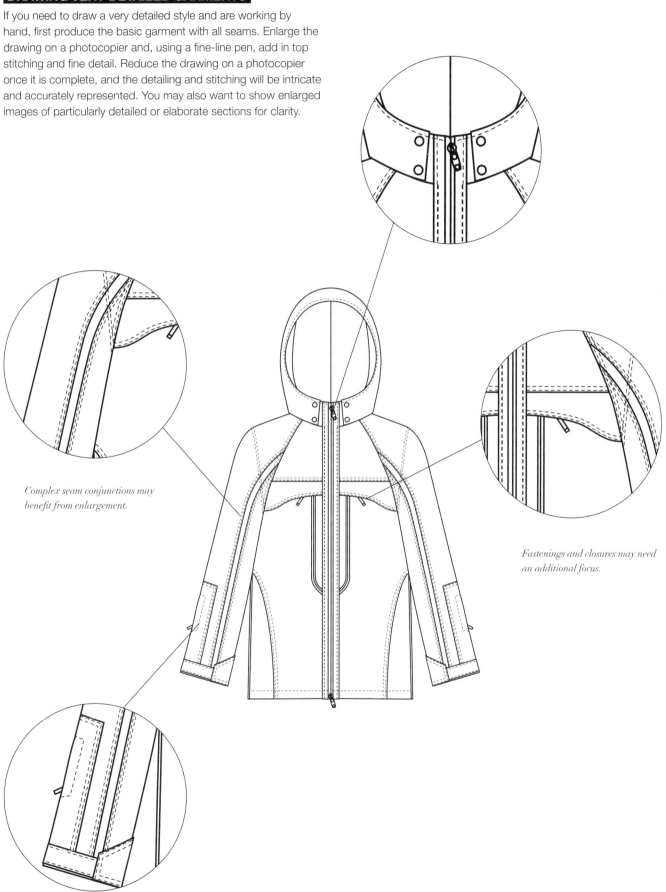

Complex seam conjunctions may benefit from enlargement.

Fastenings and closures may need an additional focus.

ADDING COLOUR, TEXTURE AND PATTERNS TO TECHNICAL DRAWINGS

Once you have completed your technical drawings, including all the detailing, they may then be rendered to show the colour, texture or pattern of the fabric or material if required. Technical drawings are usually left unrendered when used on design development sheets, presentation sheets, spec sheets, costing sheets, pattern books, pricelists and look books, but may be rendered on range boards, or when it is necessary to show such detail as different colourways, fabrics or textures, for example. Colouring-up is usually undertaken in Photoshop.

BLOCK COLOUR

Most colouring-up will involve the application of block colour.

STEP 1

You can either scan in a hand-drawn technical drawing or work from a drawing created in Illustrator. Whichever route you choose, the drawing should be imported in to Photoshop.

STEP 2

Select the panels you wish to colour-up and use the Paint Bucket Tool to add colour.

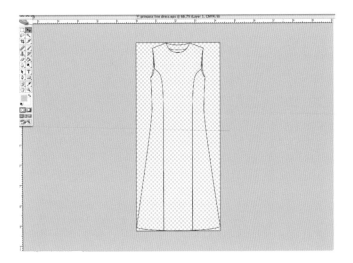

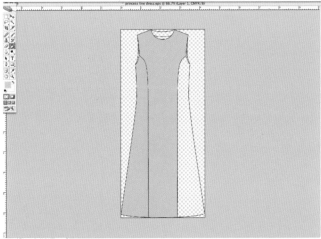

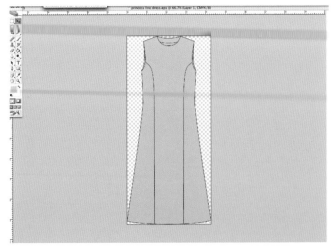

If you have a complicated garment – one with lots of gathers, for example, it can be more difficult to colour-up, as the Paint Bucket Tool may not fill in all of the individual pixels (see below and below left, close-up detail).

In this case you can either use the Paint Bucket Tool or Pencil Tool to fill in the colour.

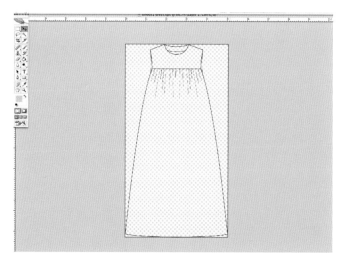

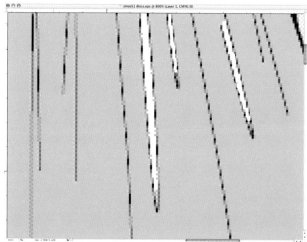

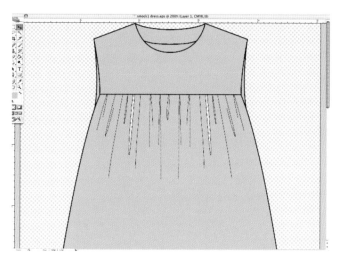

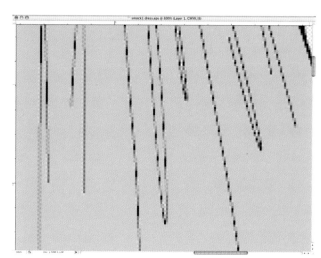

Alternatively, you can fill a selection with a background colour by holding down the Apple/Control key and pressing the Backspace key. To fill with a foreground colour, hold down the Alt key and press Backspace. This will fill the entire block without the need to colour in pixels individually.

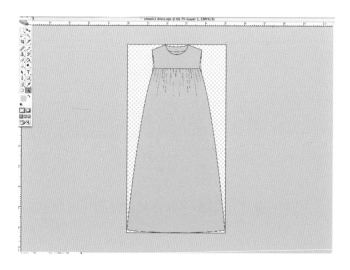

PATTERN

When applying print or pattern to a style, pay attention to where the seams and gathers are, as these will cause a break in the pattern. Do not simply lay a pattern flat over a garment, as it would not look this way in real life. You also need to consider the scale of your print pattern to ensure an accurate representation.

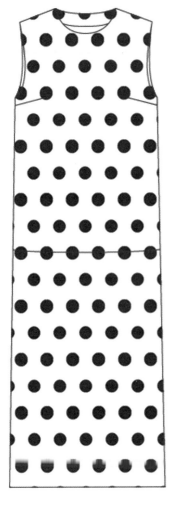

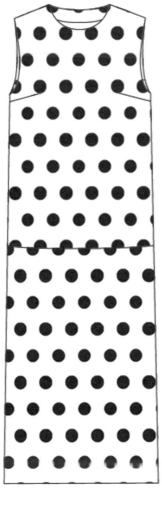

Unless the texture of a fabric is very different (fake fur, for example), the drawing will stay the same. Texture will occasionally vary the line of a technical drawing, as seen in the example below: the style is shown as though it were made in a simple calico cotton (left), and then in a short-pile fake-fur fabric (right).

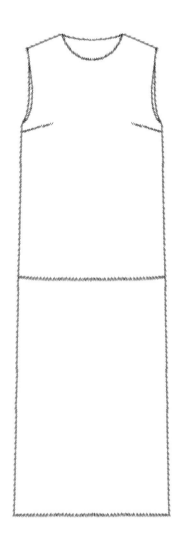

DIFFERENT DRAWING STYLES

It is inevitable that your technical drawing will be in your own specific style. As long as the technical drawing is clear, detailed and in proportion, it is acceptable that it retains your own personal signature.

Shown here are a number of interpretations by different hands of the same single-breasted jacket. Note the differences as well as the similarities. We all see things differently, however the key to a successful technical drawing is an understanding of proportion, styling, and garment construction.

STYLING DETAILS

To produce a technical drawing, a knowledge of basic styling information may be used as a guide. The outlines on the following pages are a reminder of terminology and the standard elements for a skirt, trouser, shirt and jacket. The diagrams on pages 56–59 show how to interpret different sleeve-, dress-, skirt-, trouser- and coat lengths on the generic template.

BASIC SKIRT

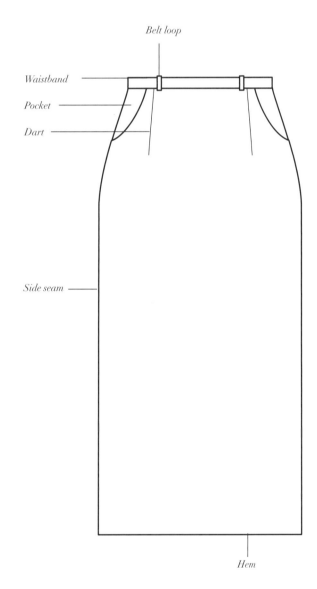

Front view

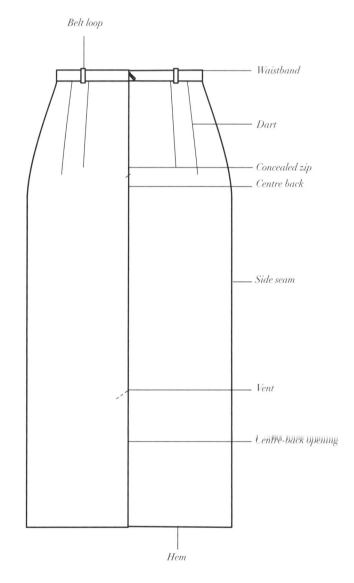

Back view

BASIC TROUSER

Fly front showing internal detail

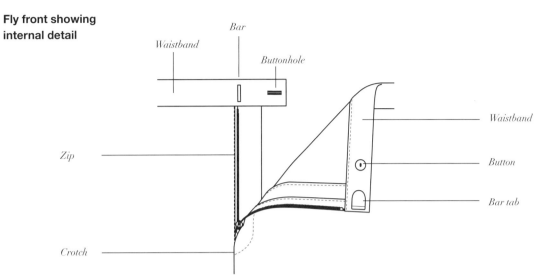

Waistband

Bar

Buttonhole

Zip

Waistband

Button

Bar tab

Crotch

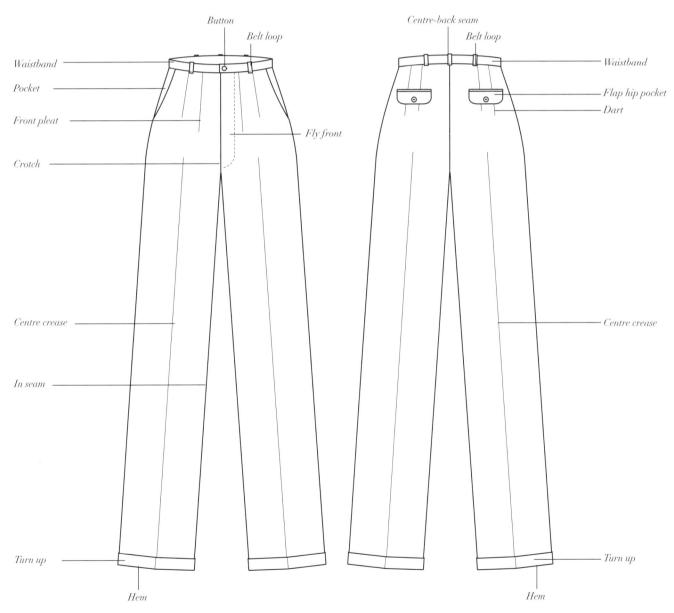

Button

Belt loop

Waistband

Pocket

Front pleat

Crotch

Fly front

Centre-back seam

Belt loop

Waistband

Flap hip pocket

Dart

Centre crease

Centre crease

In seam

Turn up

Turn up

Hem

Hem

Front view

Back view

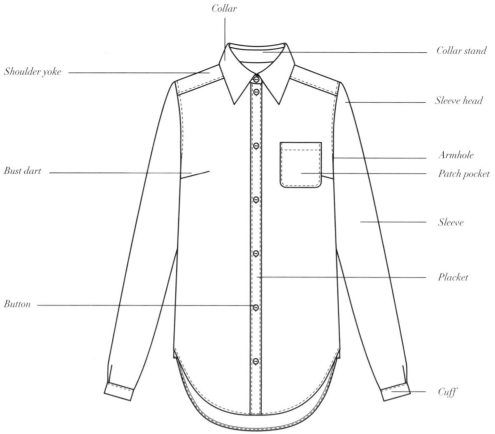

Collar

Shoulder yoke

Bust dart

Button

Collar stand

Sleeve head

Armhole

Patch pocket

Sleeve

Placket

Cuff

Front view

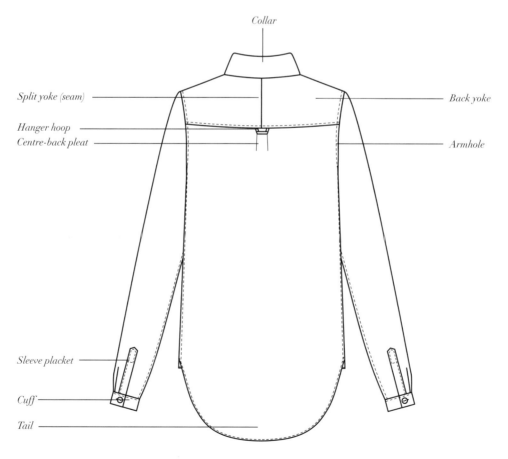

Collar

Split yoke (seam)

Hanger hoop

Centre-back pleat

Back yoke

Armhole

Sleeve placket

Cuff

Tail

Back view

Loop

Back facing

Sleeve head

Armhole

2-piece sleeve

Dart

Pocket

Collar

Rever

Welt pocket

Button

Buttonhole

Side seam

Seam

Sleeve hem

Hem

Front view

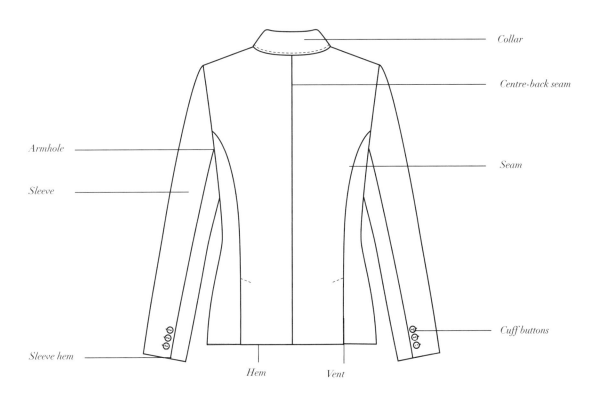

Collar

Centre-back seam

Armhole

Sleeve

Seam

Cuff buttons

Sleeve hem

Hem

Vent

Back view

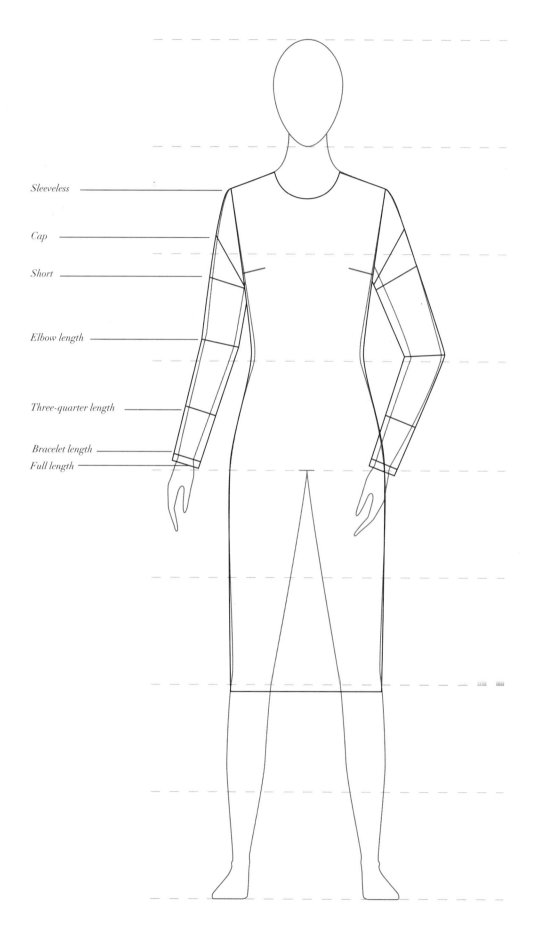

Sleeveless

Cap

Short

Elbow length

Three-quarter length

Bracelet length

Full length

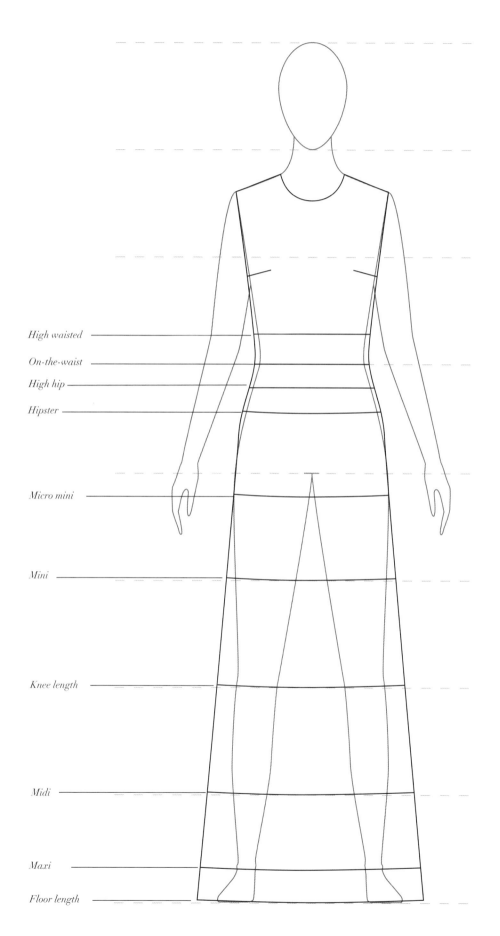

High waisted

On-the-waist

High hip

Hipster

Micro mini

Mini

Knee length

Midi

Maxi

Floor length

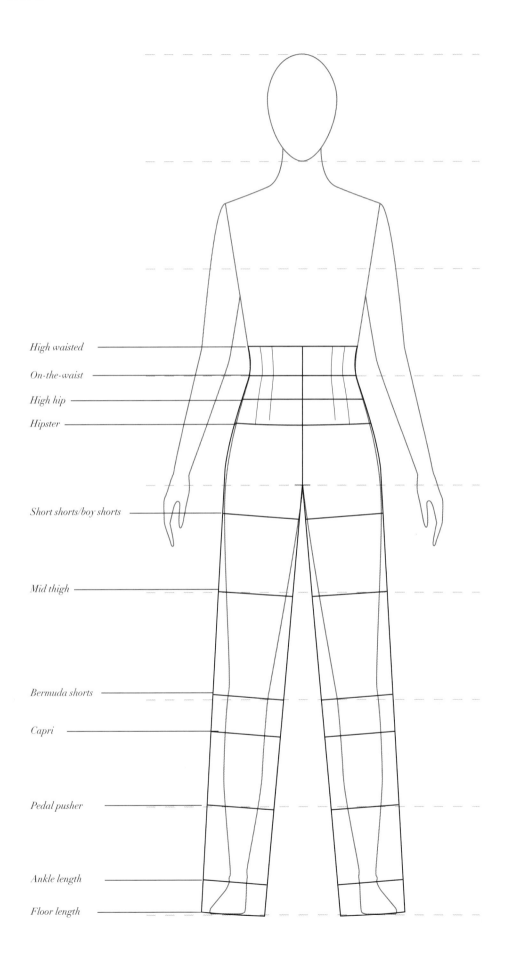

High waisted

On-the-waist

High hip

Hipster

Short shorts/boy shorts

Mid thigh

Bermuda shorts

Capri

Pedal pusher

Ankle length

Floor length

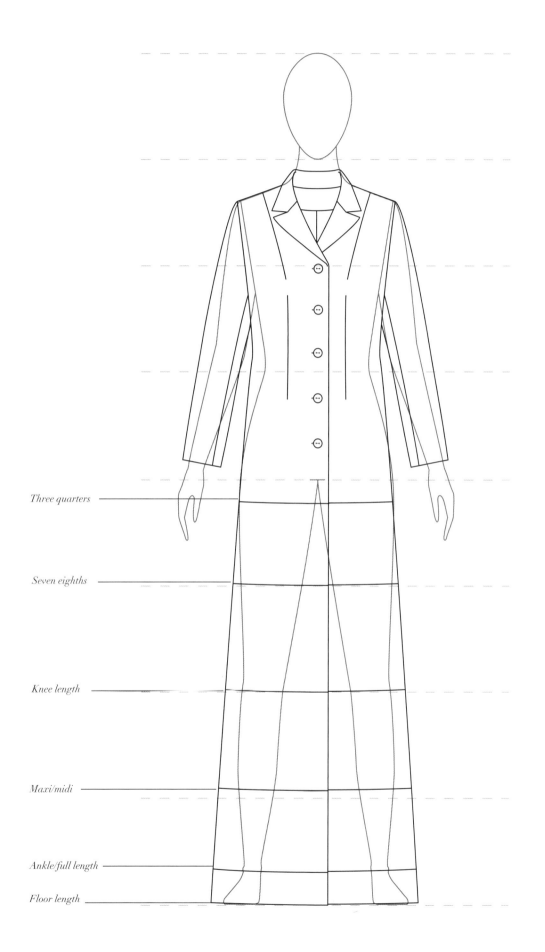

Three quarters

Seven eighths

Knee length

Maxi/midi

Ankle/full length

Floor length

VISUAL DIRECTORY
OF STYLES
AND DETAILS

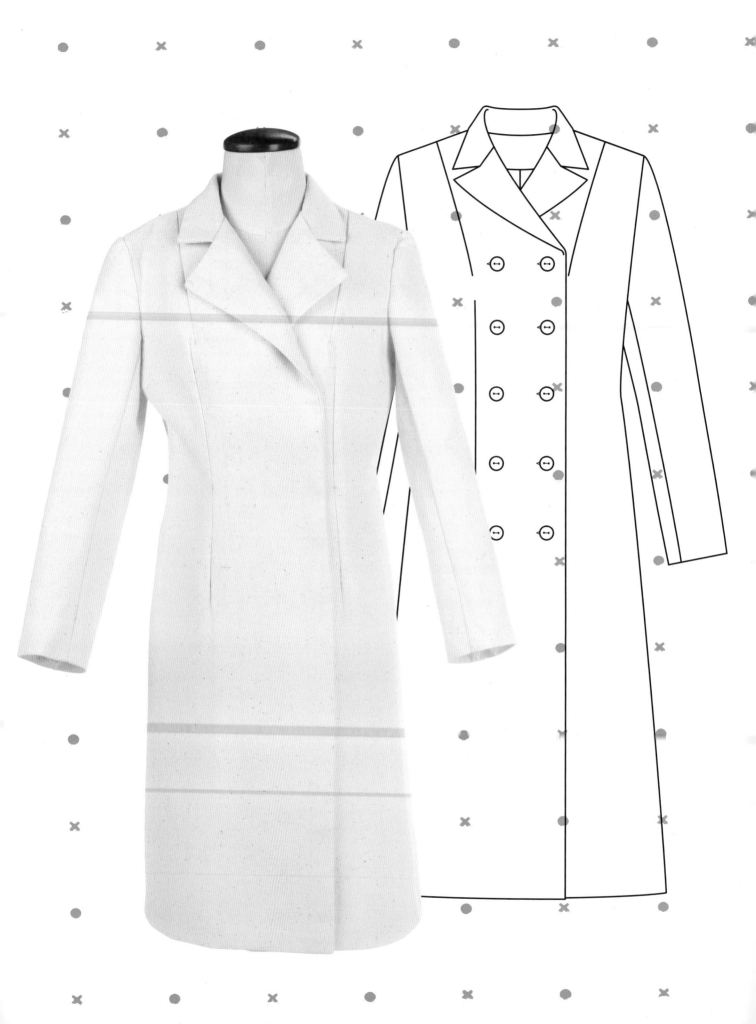

USING THE DIRECTORY

This section of the book is a selection of key shapes and garments for womenswear. The main garment groups have been researched and analyzed to create a core collection of generic known styles. 'Fashion' details have been erased, where possible, to create 'absolute' styles with the minimum of distracting details.

This directory of garment shapes is intended as a guide to the most familiar basic, classic styles and details that can be adapted and integrated into your own design ideas. There are myriad more dress, jacket, collar, skirt and trouser styles, but those featured here are the most well known.

Each garment group begins with a selection of key basic shapes, which are shown as a simple toile and as a technical drawing to demonstrate how a three-dimensional garment can translate into a two-dimensional drawing. You will learn how to visualize the garment in two dimensions, and see what needs to be left in and what should be taken out. It is key to develop a good eye in order to produce a successful technical drawing that really and truly replicates the garment design and provides essential information for anyone that looks at it.

Each style has been given the most commonly used name in industry, and you will see that sometimes there are a number of names or definitions for the same style. Understanding and becoming familiar with terminology will help you to 'speak fashion' and provide you with additional knowledge.

It is essential to become familiar with generic garments and their key components in order to develop your own styles. Try producing 100 versions of a single-breasted jacket or a double-breasted coat using your knowledge of silhouettes that 'work'. Consider sleeve types, collar options and style lines. The possibilities are endless. By starting with understood basics, you can progress to creating new undefined styles.

Go to the womenswear department of any department store, where you can make notes with ease, and see how many 'classic' collars, sleeves, cuffs, skirts and dress silhouettes you can find. And look at the multitude of variations. You will see that most garments fall into the categories listed in this section of the book. Almost everything you will see is a variation on a traditional style.

Try an experiment: using the generic template, consider how you would create a 'new' style. What will be the overall silhouette? What kind of a sleeve will it have? What about a cuff? Consider a collar? How long will it be? Combine the different elements, using the basic styles as a foundation on which to build. Design is all about variation – you will find the art of 'design development', as well as 'drawing', easier to get to grips with if you possess the building blocks.

This section provides all the information you need to get started.

KEY BASIC SHAPES

FITTED/TUBE/SHEATH
FRONT VIEW

DRESSES

FITTED/TUBE/SHEATH
BACK VIEW

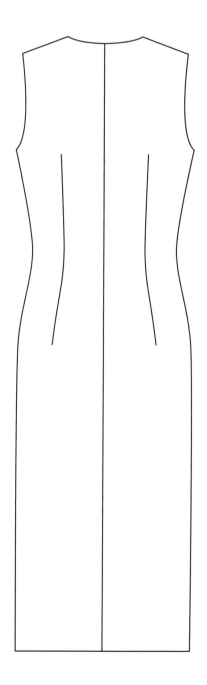

KEY BASIC SHAPES

SHIFT/TANK/CHEMISE
FRONT VIEW

DRESSES

SHIFT/TANK/CHEMISE
BACK VIEW

KEY BASIC SHAPES

A-LINE
FRONT VIEW

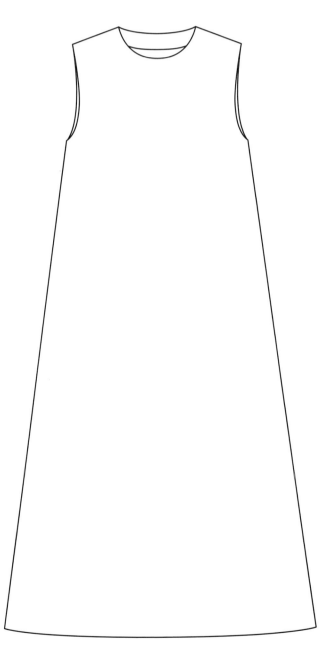

A-LINE
BACK VIEW

VARIATIONS

FRONT VIEWS
EMPIRE LINE

PRINCESS/PRINCESS LINE

TRAPEZE

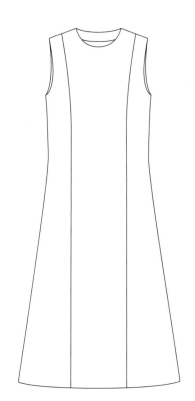

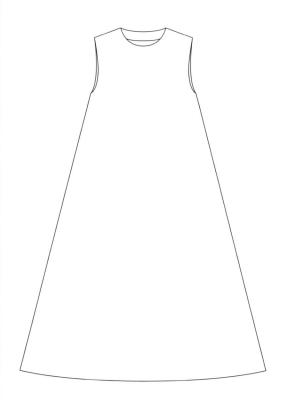

BACK VIEWS

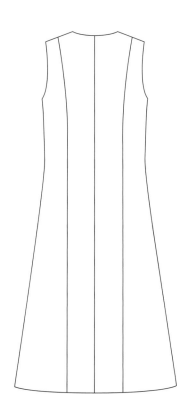

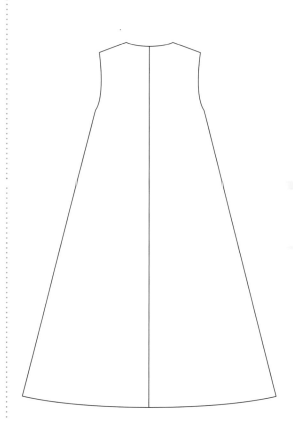

DRESSES

FRONT VIEWS
ASYMMETRIC

DROPPED WAIST/ DROP WAIST

BLOUSON

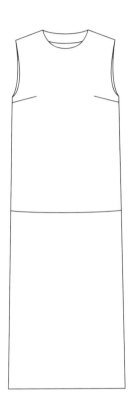

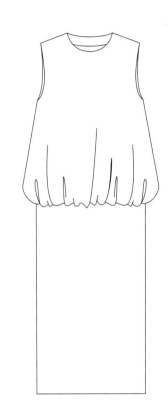

BACK VIEWS

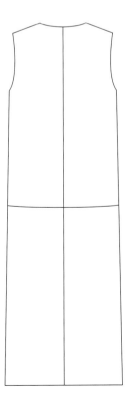

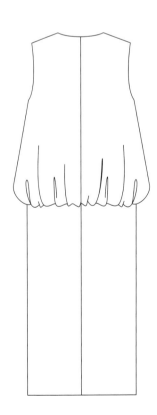

VARIATIONS

FRONT VIEWS
SMOCK

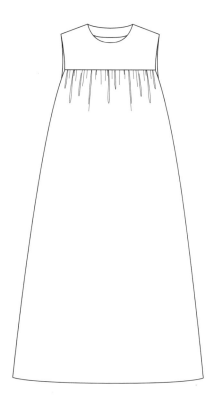

WRAPOVER/WRAP DRESS

BACK VIEWS

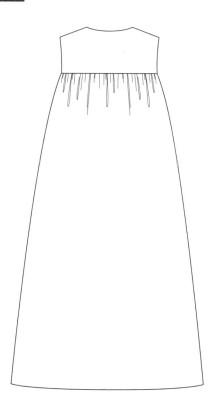

DRESSES

SHIRT DRESS

CHEONGSAM/CHINESE DRESS

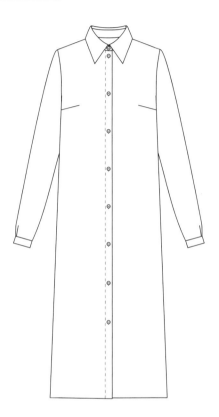

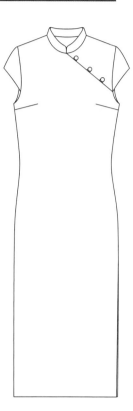

BACK VIEWS

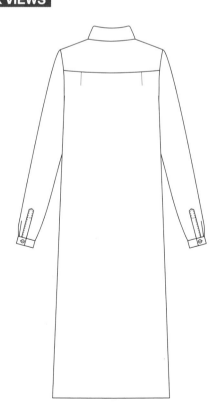

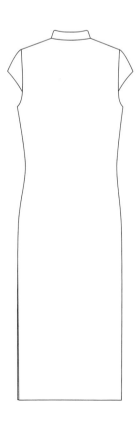

VARIATIONS

FRONT VIEWS
APRON/PINAFORE

KIMONO

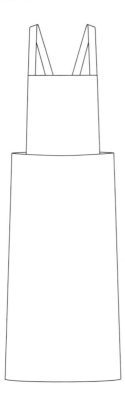

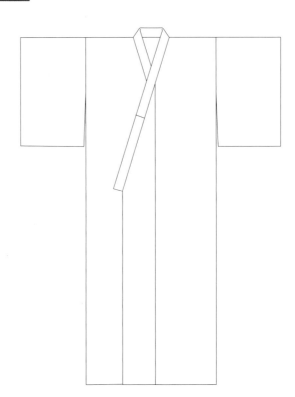

BACK VIEWS

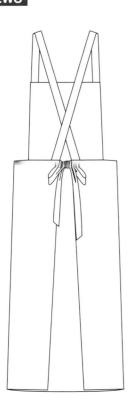

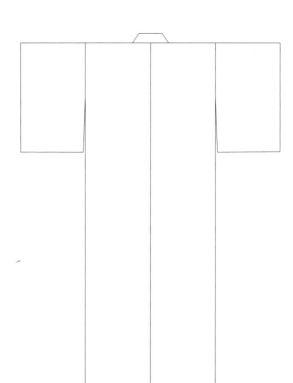

DRESSES

FRONT VIEWS

KAFTAN

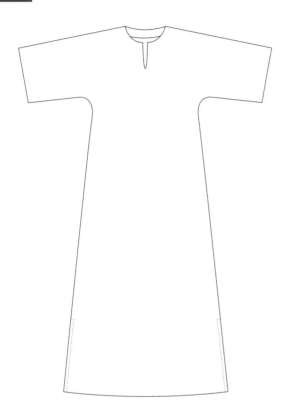

BACK VIEWS

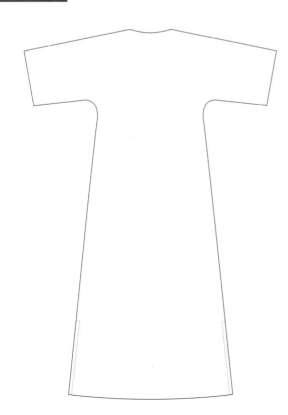

BALL GOWN/GOWN/PROM DRESS

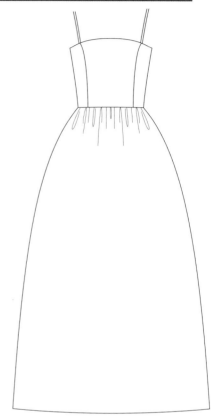

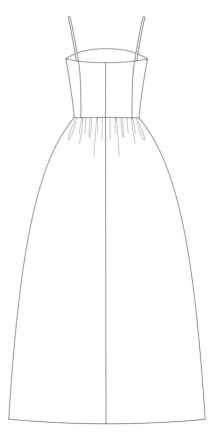

KEY BASIC SHAPES

PENCIL SKIRT/FITTED SKIRT/SHEATH
FRONT VIEW

SKIRTS

PENCIL SKIRT/FITTED SKIRT/SHEATH
BACK VIEW

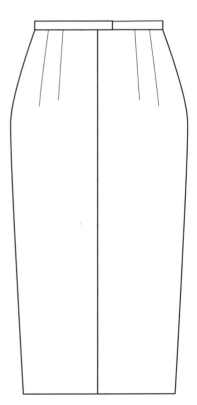

KEY BASIC SHAPES

STRAIGHT SKIRT
FRONT VIEW

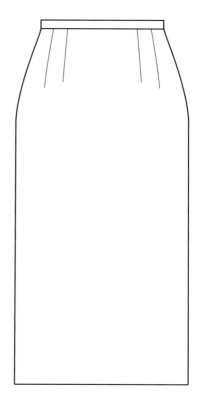

SKIRTS

STRAIGHT SKIRT
BACK VIEW

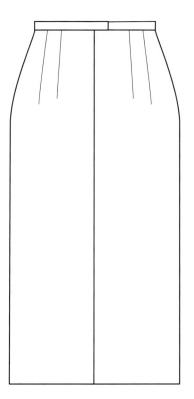

KEY BASIC SHAPES

A-LINE SKIRT
FRONT VIEW

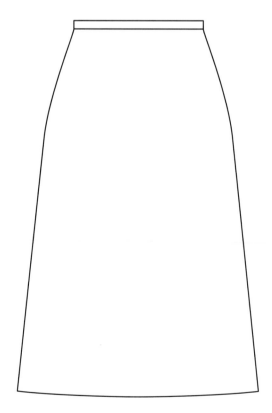

A-LINE SKIRT
BACK VIEW

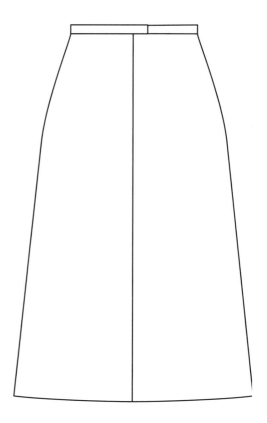

KEY BASIC SHAPES

CIRCULAR/FULL CIRCLE SKIRT
FRONT VIEW

SKIRTS

CIRCULAR/FULL CIRCLE SKIRT
BACK VIEW

KEY BASIC SHAPES

GATHERED SKIRT
FRONT VIEW

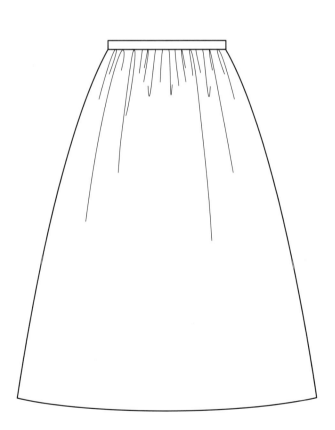

SKIRTS

GATHERED SKIRT
BACK VIEW

KEY BASIC SHAPES

PLEATED SKIRT
FRONT VIEW

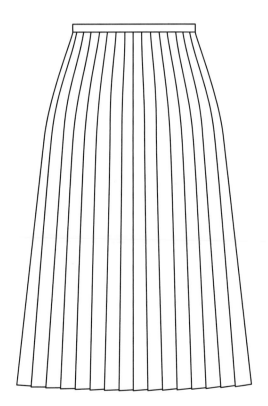

PLEATED SKIRT
BACK VIEW

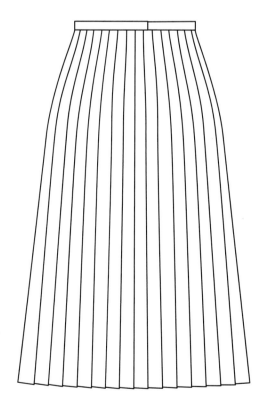

VARIATIONS

FRONT VIEWS

DIRNDL SKIRT

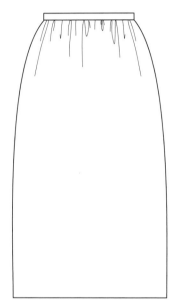

GORED SKIRT

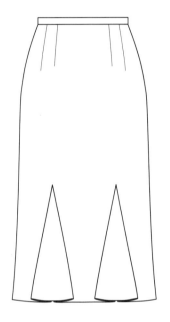

WRAP/WRAPOVER SKIRT

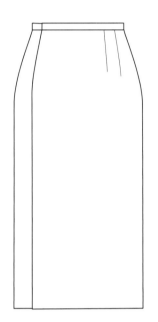

BACK VIEWS

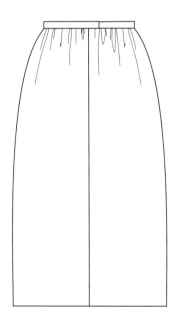

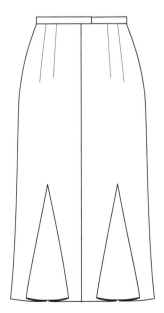

SKIRTS

FRONT VIEWS

SARONG/PAREO

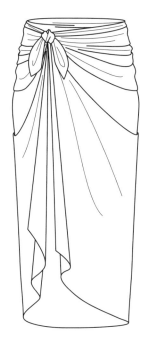

TIERED/PEASANT SKIRT

**HANDKERCHIEF HEM/
IRREGULAR HEM**

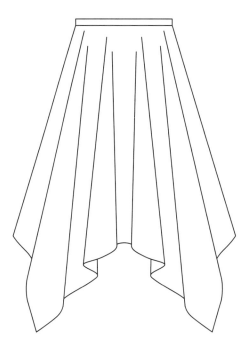

BACK VIEWS

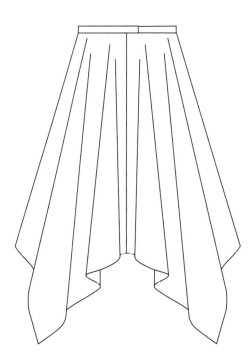

VARIATIONS

FRONT VIEWS

ASYMMETRIC SKIRT

PUFFBALL/BUBBLE/BALLOON

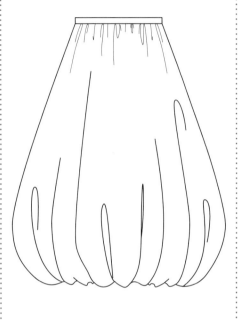

SKATING SKIRT

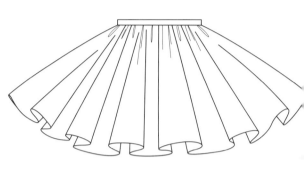

BACK VIEWS

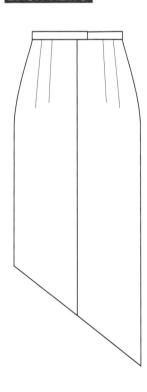

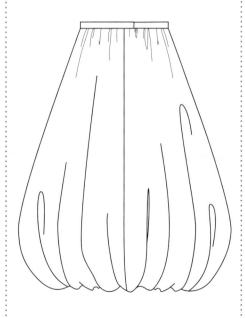

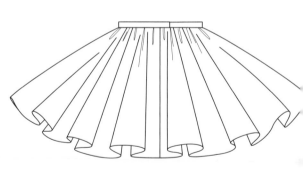

SKIRTS

KILT

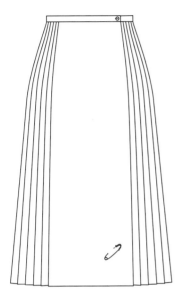

SKORT

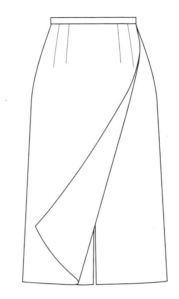

PEG/PEGGED/HOBBLE SKIRT

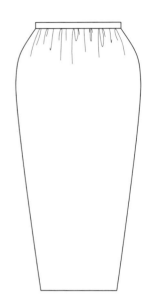

BACK VIEWS

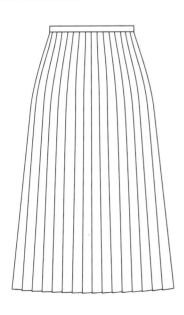

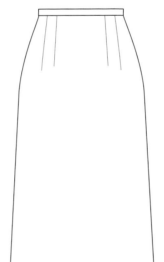

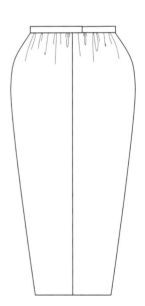

KEY BASIC SHAPES

LEGGING
FRONT VIEW

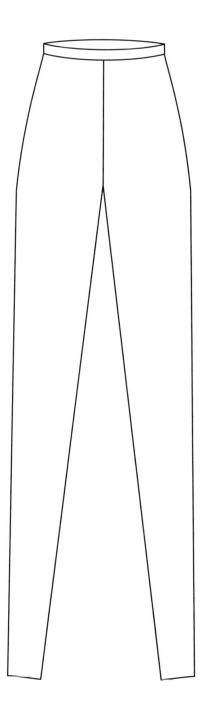

TROUSERS

LEGGING
BACK VIEW

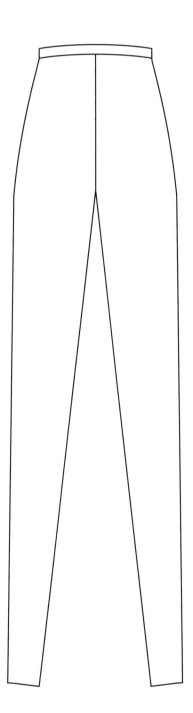

KEY BASIC SHAPES

DRAINPIPE/SKINNY/CIGARETTE PANT/STOVEPIPE
FRONT VIEW

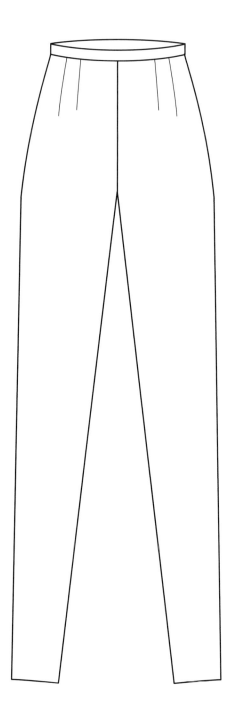

TROUSERS

DRAINPIPE/SKINNY/CIGARETTE PANT/STOVEPIPE
BACK VIEW

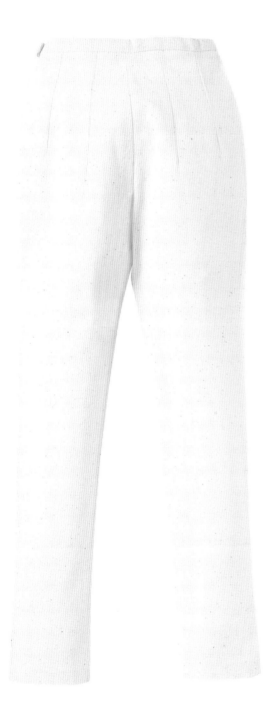

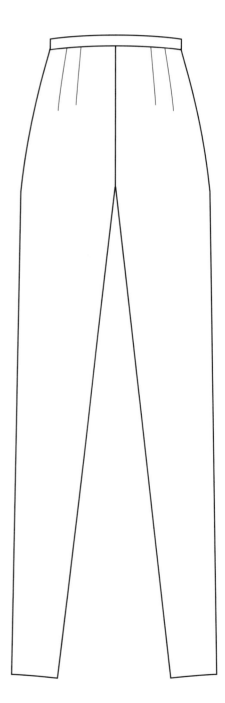

KEY BASIC SHAPES

STRAIGHT
FRONT VIEW

TROUSERS

STRAIGHT
BACK VIEW

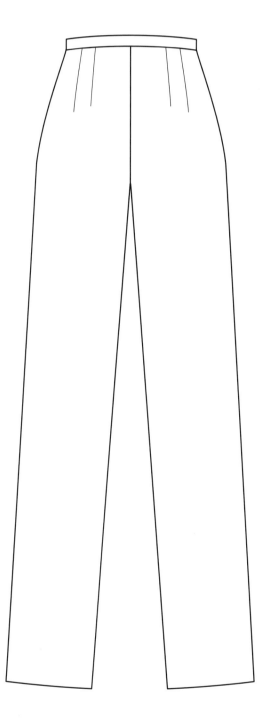

KEY BASIC SHAPES

TAPERED
FRONT VIEW

TROUSERS

TAPERED
BACK VIEW

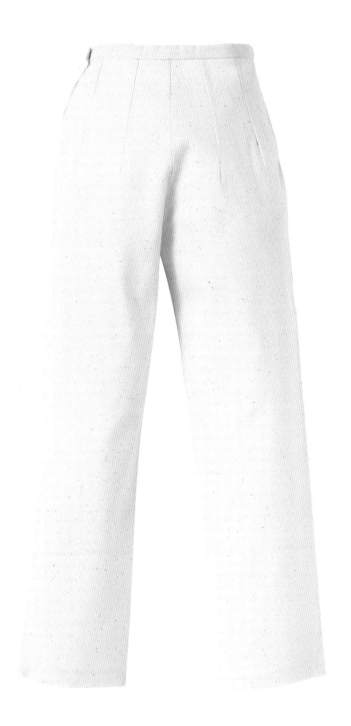

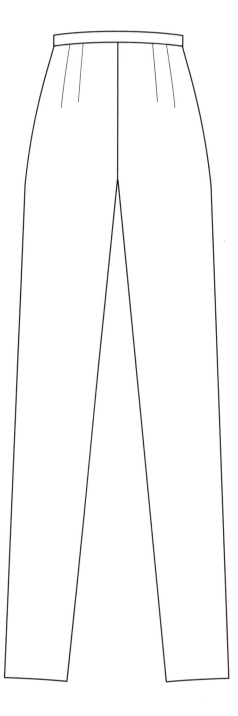

KEY BASIC SHAPES

....

BELLBOTTOM/FLARE
FRONT VIEW

TROUSERS

BELLBOTTOM/FLARE
BACK VIEW

VARIATIONS

FRONT VIEWS
BOOTLEG/BOOTCUT

JEAN/JEANS

CARGO PANT/COMBAT TROUSER

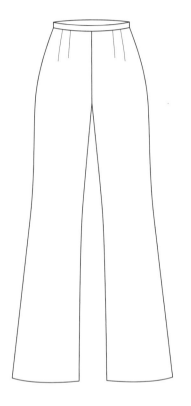

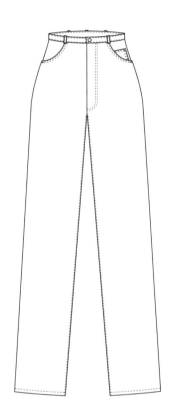

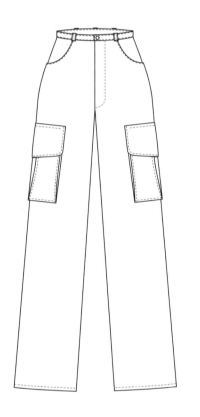

BACK VIEWS

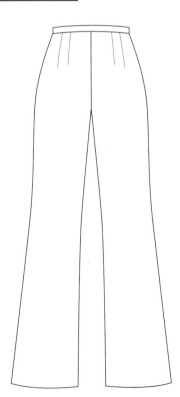

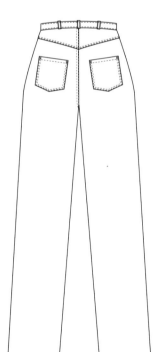

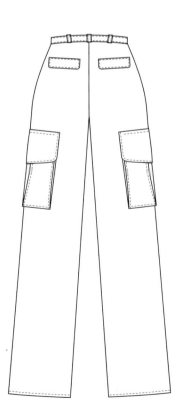

TROUSERS

OXFORD BAG

JODHPUR/RIDING PANT

PALAZZO PANT

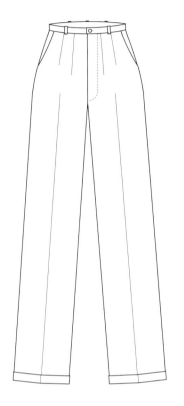
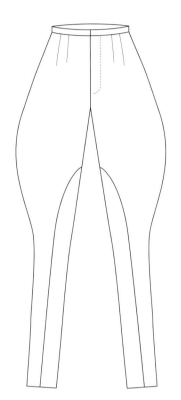
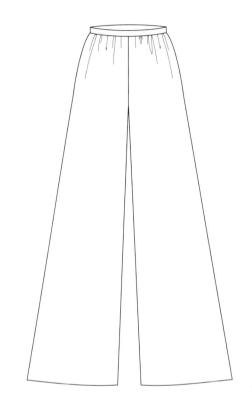

BACK VIEWS

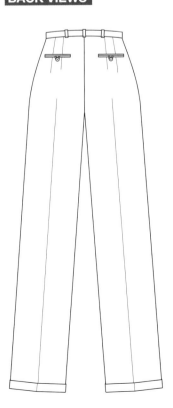
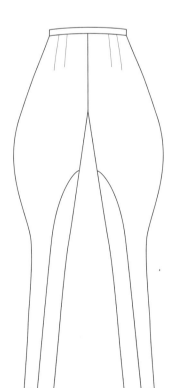
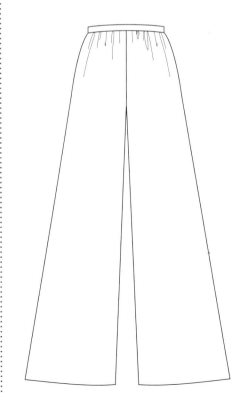

VARIATIONS

FRONT VIEWS
SAILOR

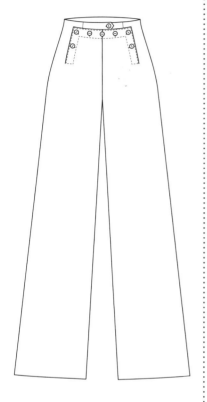

HAREM

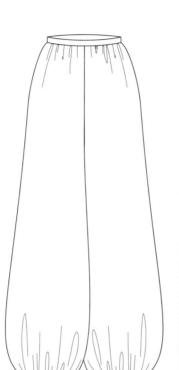

ZOUAVE

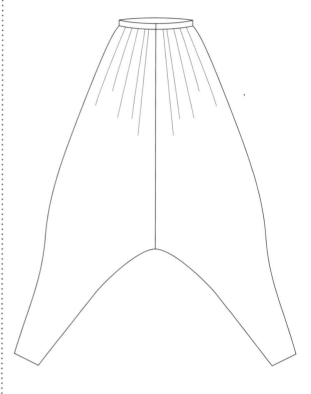

BACK VIEWS

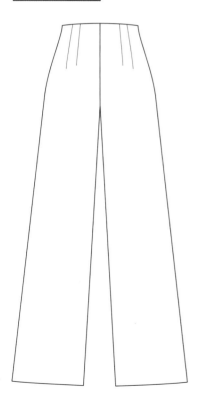

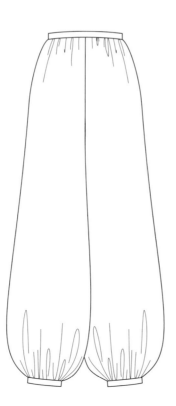

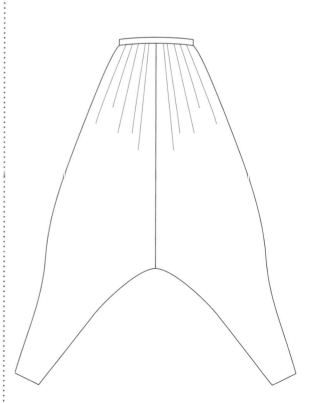

TROUSERS

DHOTI

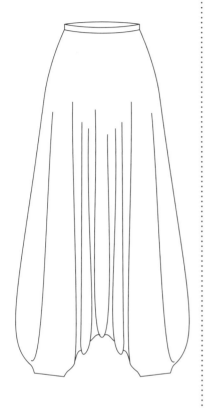

HAKAMA

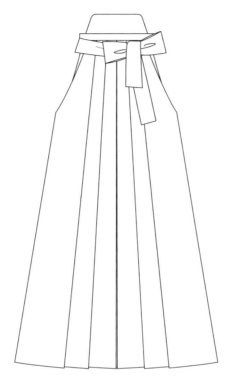

CULOTTE/TROUSER SKIRT

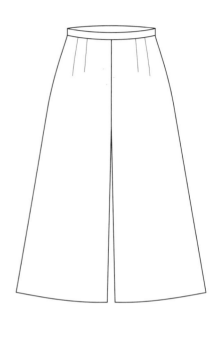

BACK VIEWS

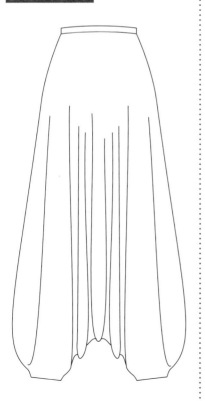

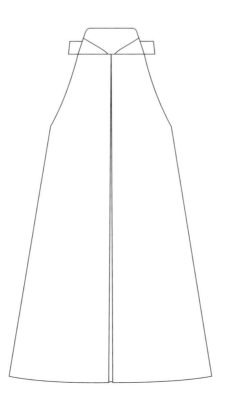

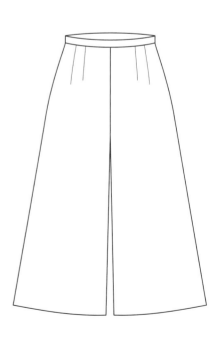

VARIATIONS

FRONT VIEWS
HOTPANT/MICRO SHORT/
SHORT SHORTS

BLOOMER

BOXER SHORT

BACK VIEWS

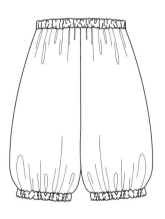

TROUSERS

BERMUDA SHORT

KNICKERBOCKER

GOUCHO PANT

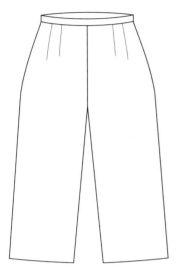

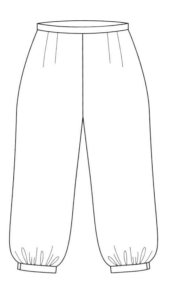

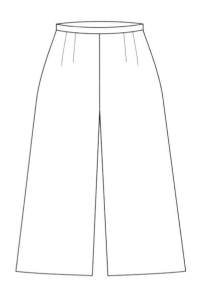

BACK VIEWS

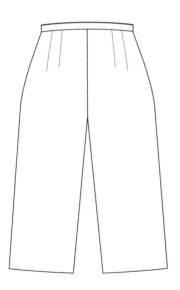

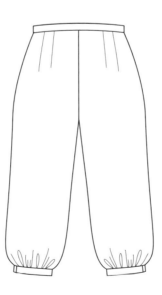

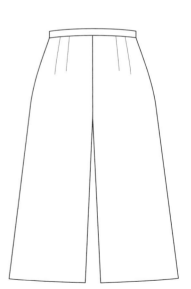

VARIATIONS

FRONT VIEWS
CAPRI/SABRINA PANT

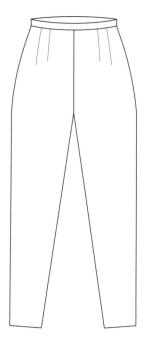

PEDAL PUSHER/CLAM DIGGER

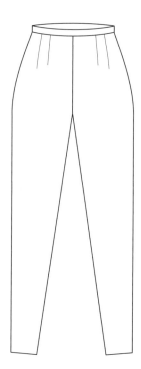

BACK VIEWS

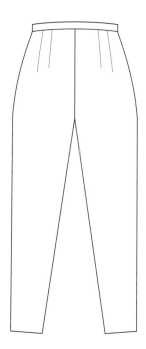

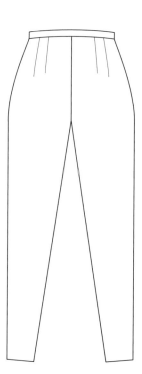

TROUSERS

FRONT VIEWS
JOGGER/SWEAT PANT/TRACK PANT

PLAYSUIT/ROMPER SUIT

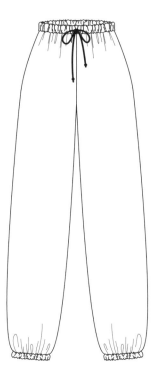

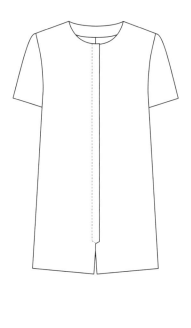

BACK VIEWS

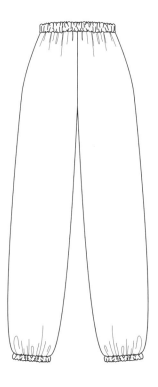

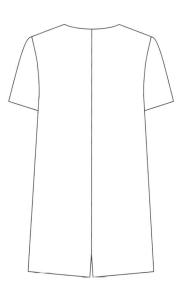

VARIATIONS

FRONT VIEWS
DUNGAREE/BIB OVERALL

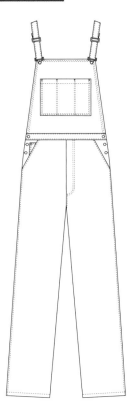

JUMPSUIT/BOILER SUIT/OVERALL

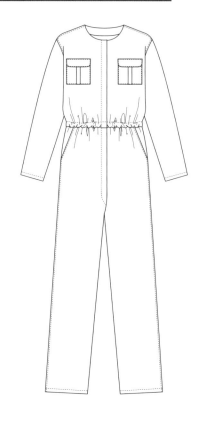

BACK VIEWS

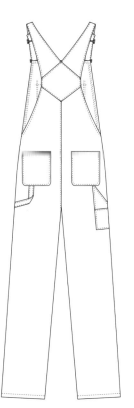

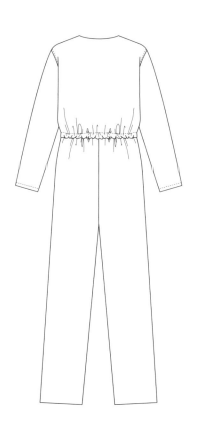

TROUSERS

ALL-IN-ONE BODY SUIT/CATSUIT/UNITARD

STIRRUP PANT

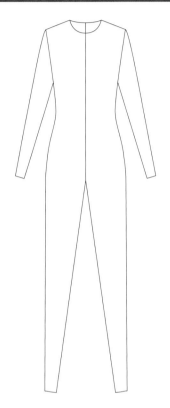

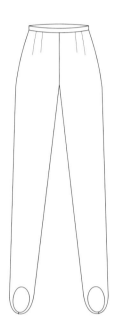

BACK VIEWS

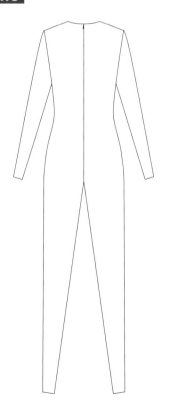

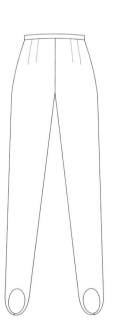

KEY BASIC SHAPES

CAMISOLE/STRAPPY VEST
FRONT VIEW

TOPS

CAMISOLE/STRAPPY VEST
BACK VIEW

KEY BASIC SHAPES

VEST/TANK
FRONT VIEW

TOPS

VEST/TANK
BACK VIEW

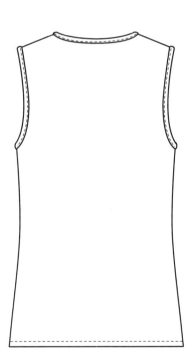

KEY BASIC SHAPES

TUNIC
FRONT VIEW

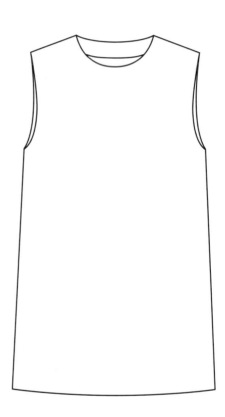

TOPS

TUNIC
BACK VIEW

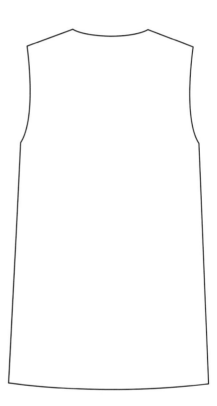

KEY BASIC SHAPES

T-SHIRT/TEE
FRONT VIEW

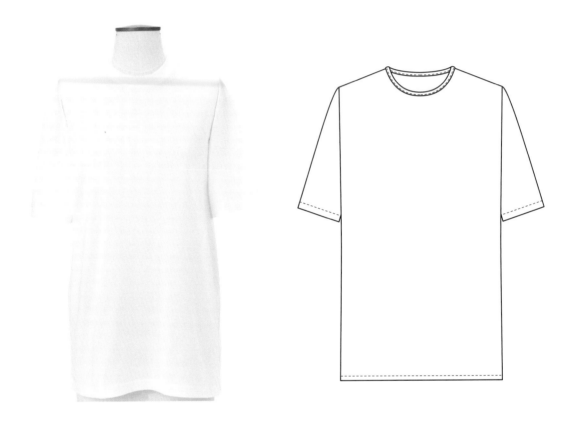

T-SHIRT/TEE
BACK VIEW

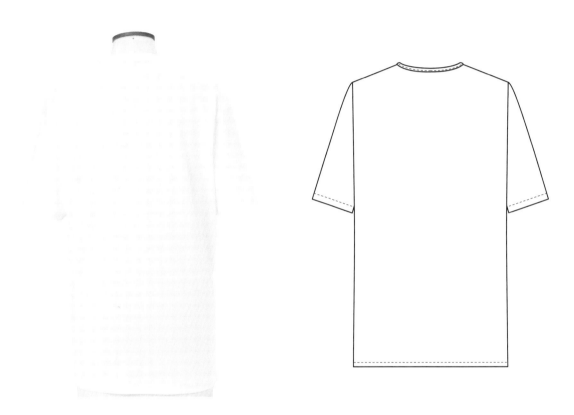

KEY BASIC SHAPES

SHIRT
FRONT VIEW

TOPS

SHIRT
BACK VIEW

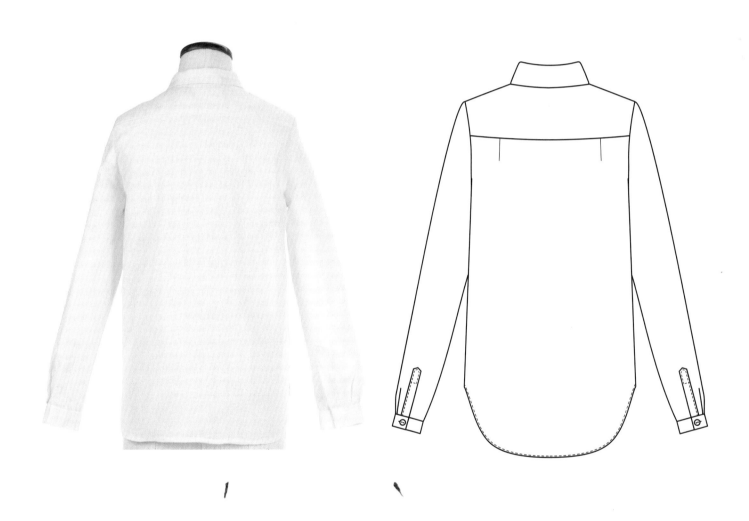

VARIATIONS

FRONT VIEWS
CROP/MIDRIFF TOP

SLEEVELESS T-SHIRT

WAISTCOAT

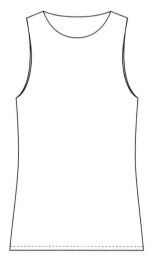

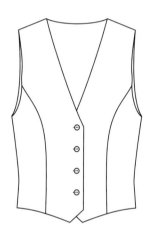

BACK VIEWS

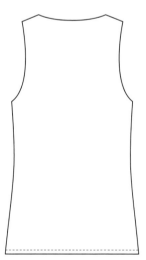

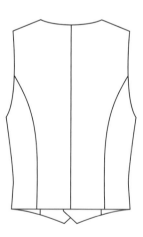

TOPS

CARDIGAN

BLOUSE

**STRAPLESS TOP/
BOOB TUBE**

BACK VIEWS

VARIATIONS

FRONT VIEWS
BUSTIER

CORSET

HALTER/HALTER NECK

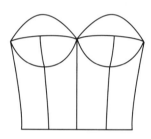

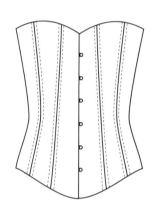

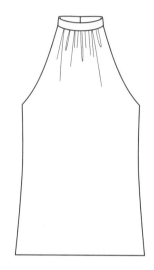

BACK VIEWS

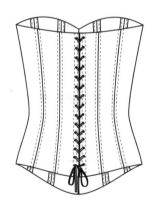

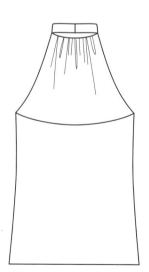

TOPS

FRONT VIEWS

COSSACK

GYPSY/PEASANT BLOUSE

BLOUSON

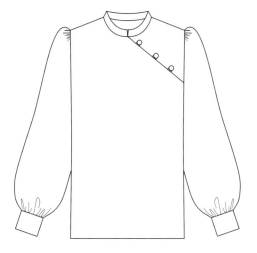

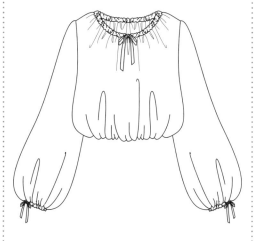

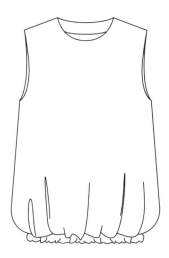

BACK VIEWS

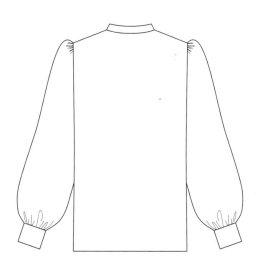

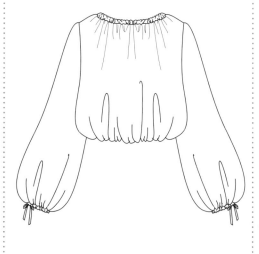

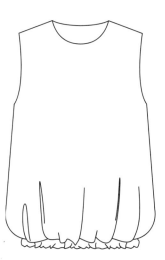

VARIATIONS

FRONT VIEWS
WRAP TOP/BALLET TOP

KURTA/KURTI

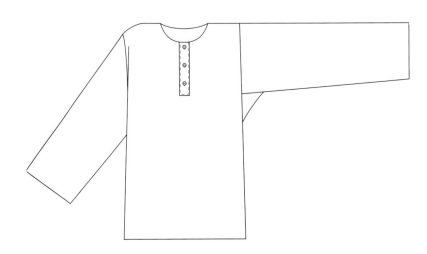

BACK VIEWS

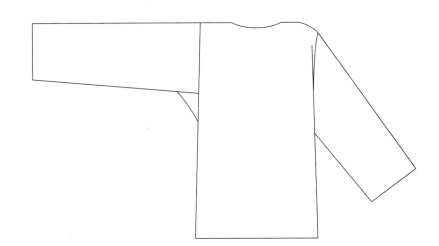

TOPS

POLO SHIRT **SWEATSHIRT/JOGGING TOP/SWEAT TOP** **BODYSUIT/BODY**

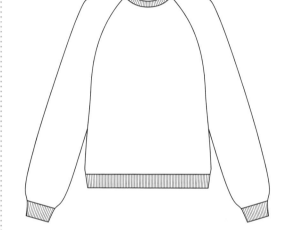
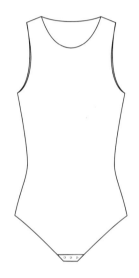

BACK VIEWS

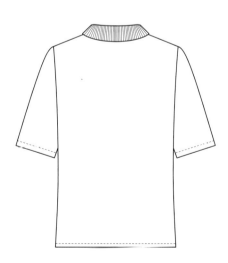
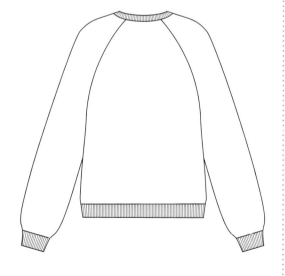
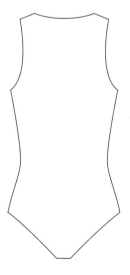

KEY BASIC SHAPES

CLASSIC SINGLE-BREASTED
FRONT VIEW

JACKETS

CLASSIC SINGLE-BREASTED
BACK VIEW

KEY BASIC SHAPES

CLASSIC DOUBLE-BREASTED
FRONT VIEW

JACKETS

CLASSIC DOUBLE-BREASTED
BACK VIEW

KEY BASIC SHAPES

CASUAL/UNSTRUCTURED
FRONT VIEW

JACKETS

CASUAL/UNSTRUCTURED
BACK VIEW

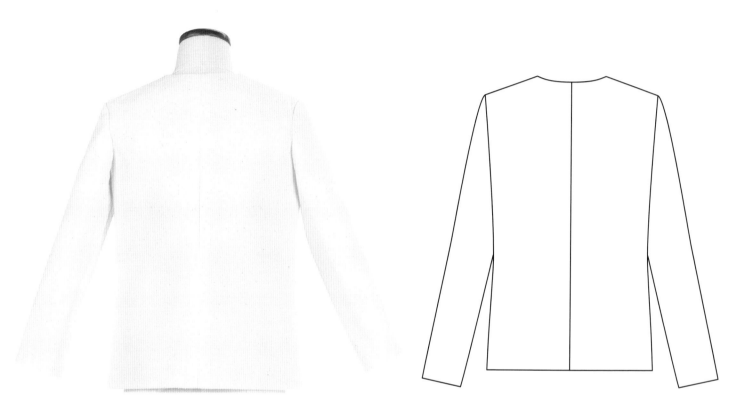

VARIATIONS

FRONT VIEWS
SHRUG

BOLERO JACKET

SPENCER JACKET

BACK VIEWS

JACKETS

BLAZER/BOX JACKET

TUXEDO/DINNER JACKET

CHINESE/MANDARIN JACKET

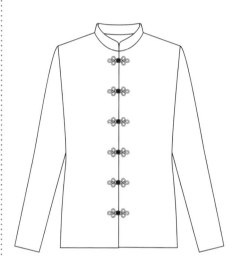

BACK VIEWS

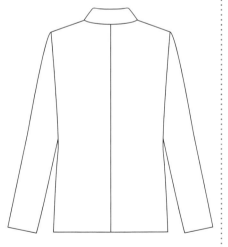

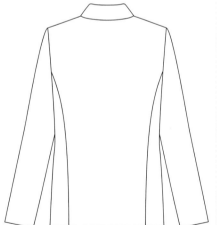

VARIATIONS

FRONT VIEWS

NEHRU JACKET

SAFARI JACKET

NORFOLK JACKET

BACK VIEWS

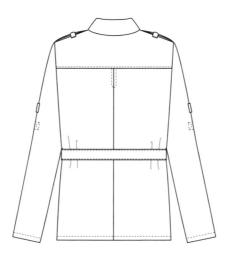

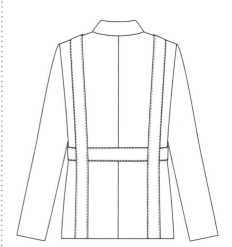

JACKETS

FRONT VIEWS
BOMBER/BLOUSON/FLIGHT JACKET

WESTERN/JEAN JACKET

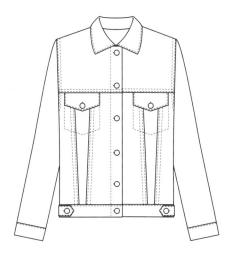

BACK VIEWS

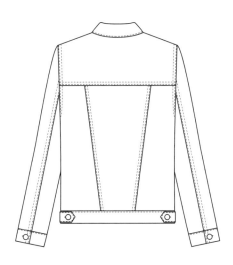

VARIATIONS

FRONT VIEWS
BIKER/MOTORCYCLE JACKET

WINDCHEATER/CAGOULE

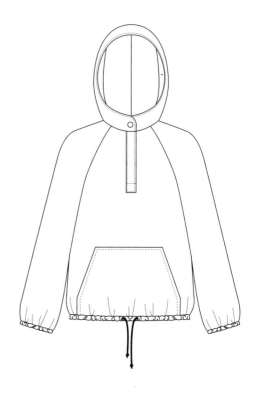

BACK VIEWS

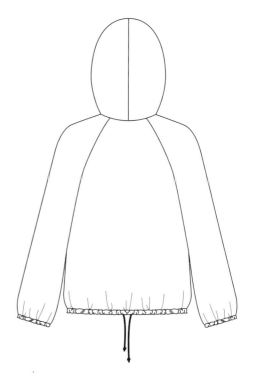

JACKETS

FRONT VIEWS
BODY WARMER/PADDED WAISTCOAT/
QUILTED VEST/PADDED GILET

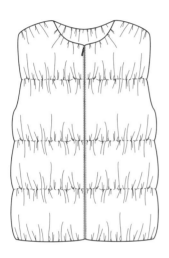

BACK VIEWS

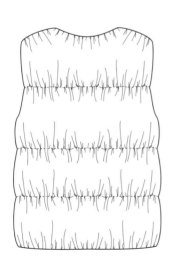

PARKA/ANORAK

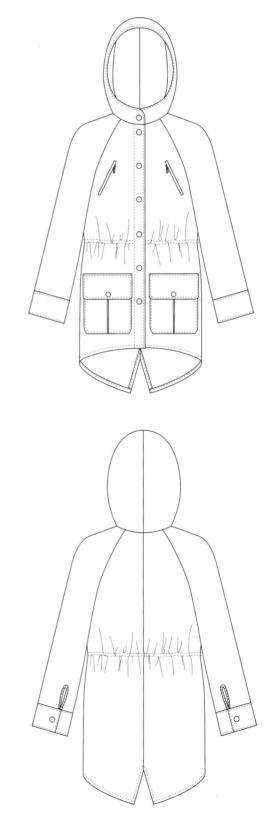

KEY BASIC SHAPES

CLASSIC SINGLE-BREASTED
FRONT VIEW

COATS

CLASSIC SINGLE-BREASTED
BACK VIEW

KEY BASIC SHAPES

. . . .

CLASSIC DOUBLE-BREASTED
FRONT VIEW

COATS

CLASSIC DOUBLE-BREASTED
BACK VIEW

KEY BASIC SHAPES

CASUAL/UNSTRUCTURED
FRONT VIEW

COATS

CASUAL/UNSTRUCTURED
BACK VIEW

VARIATIONS

FRONT VIEWS
PRINCESS/PRINCESS-LINE

MACKINTOSH/MAC

TRENCH COAT

 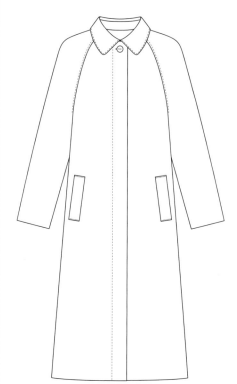 

BACK VIEWS

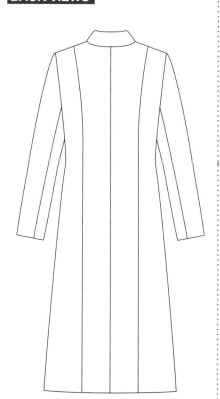 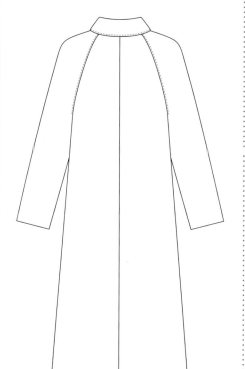 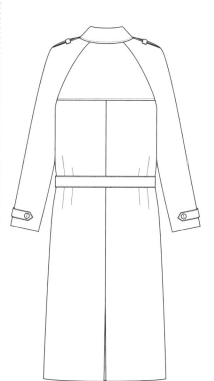

COATS

FRONT VIEWS

COCOON COAT

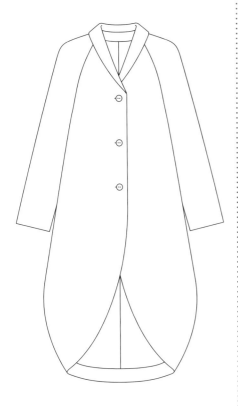

PEA COAT

SWAGGER COAT/TENT COAT

SWING COAT

BACK VIEWS

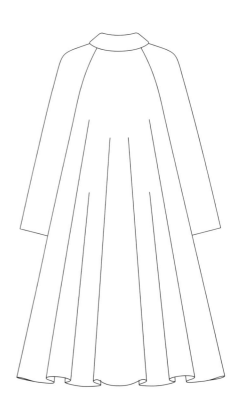

VARIATIONS

FRONT VIEWS

TAIL COAT/TAILS/MORNING COAT/CUTAWAY

DUFFLE/TOGGLE COAT

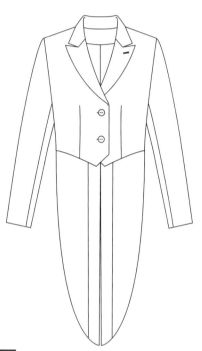

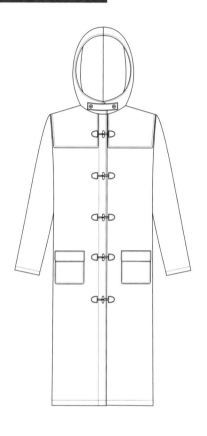

BACK VIEWS

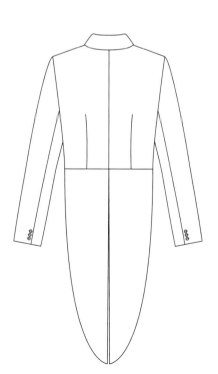

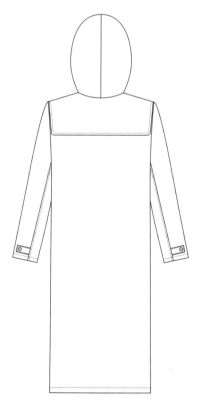

COATS

FRONT VIEWS
DUSTER COAT

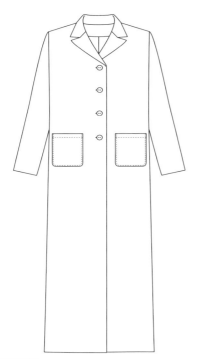

CAPE

BACK VIEWS

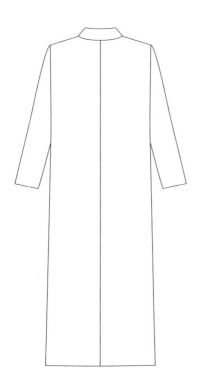

KEY BASIC SHAPES

ROUND/JEWEL NECK
FRONT VIEW

BACK VIEW

 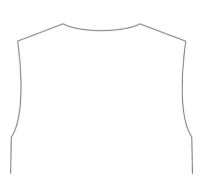

NECKLINES

BACK VIEW

 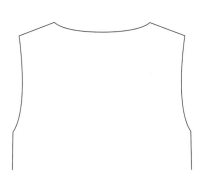

KEY BASIC SHAPES

U-NECK
FRONT VIEW

 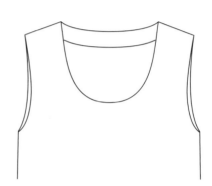

BACK VIEW

NECKLINES

SCOOP/SCOOPED NECK
FRONT VIEW

 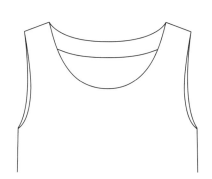

BACK VIEW

 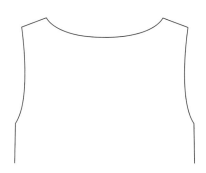

KEY BASIC SHAPES

FRONT VIEW
BOAT NECK/BATEAU NECK

 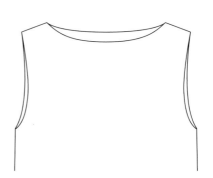

BACK VIEW

 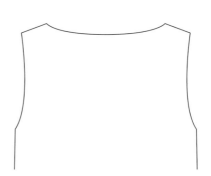

NECKLINES

SQUARE NECK
FRONT VIEW

 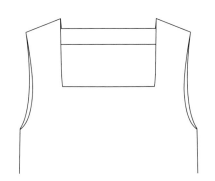

BACK VIEW

 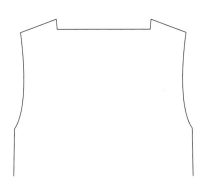

VARIATIONS

FRONT VIEWS

SLIT/PLUNGE NECK

BACK VIEWS

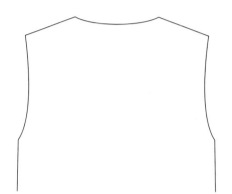

KEYHOLE

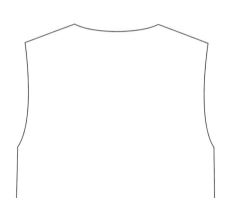

SWEETHEART

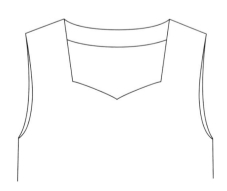
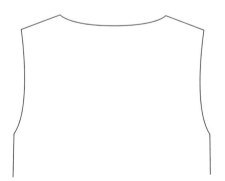

NECKLINES

ASYMMETRIC

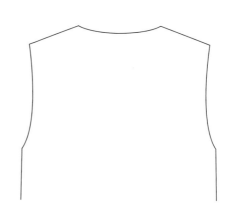

OFF-THE-SHOULDER/ONE SHOULDER

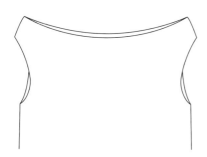

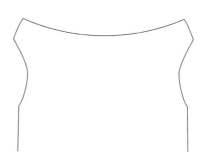

GATHERED

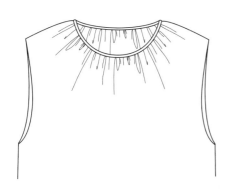

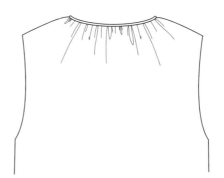

VARIATIONS

FRONT VIEWS

DRAWSTRING

CREW NECK

 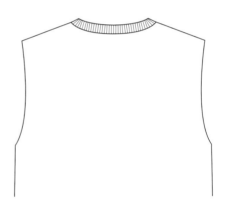

TURTLE NECK/POLO NECK

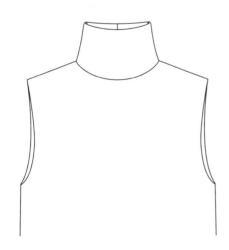 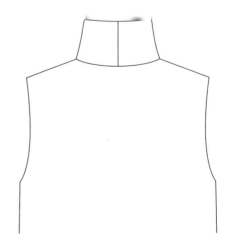

NECKLINES

FUNNEL NECK/GROWN-ON NECKLINE

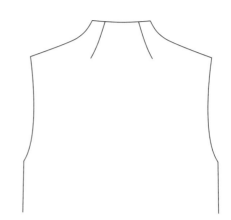

COWL NECK

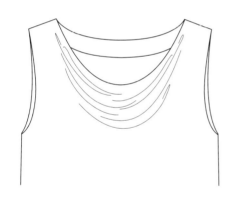
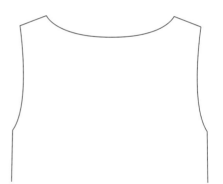

ROLL NECK

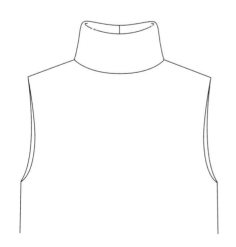
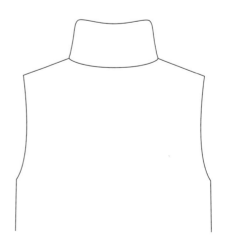

KEY BASIC SHAPES

TWO-PIECE SHIRT COLLAR/COLLAR AND BAND/TRADITIONAL COLLAR
FRONT VIEW

BACK VIEW

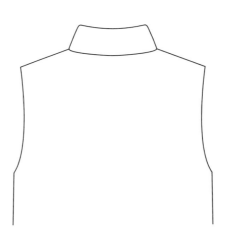

COLLARS

ONE-PIECE SHIRT COLLAR/CONVERTIBLE COLLAR
FRONT VIEW

BACK VIEW

 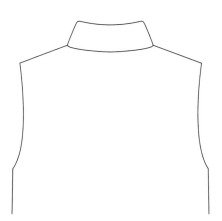

KEY BASIC SHAPES

COLLAR AND REVER/NOTCHED COLLAR
FRONT VIEW

BACK VIEW

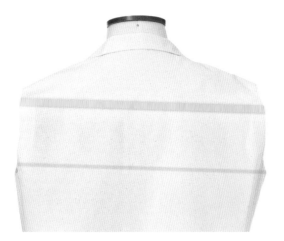
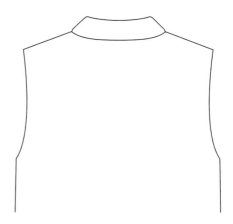

COLLARS

SHAWL COLLAR
FRONT VIEW

BACK VIEW

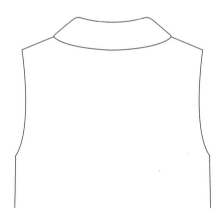

VARIATIONS

FRONT VIEWS

BACK VIEWS

BAND COLLAR/GRANDAD COLLAR

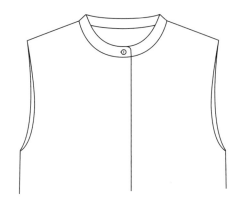 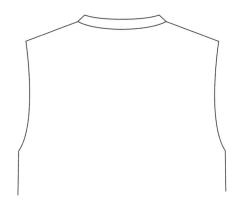

MANDARIN/CHINESE/NEHRU COLLAR

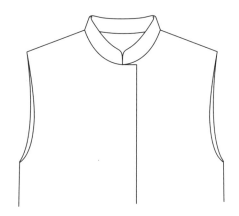 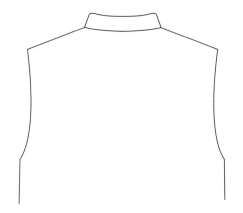

WING COLLAR

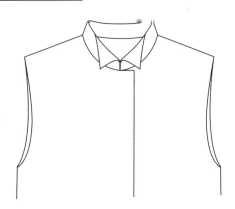 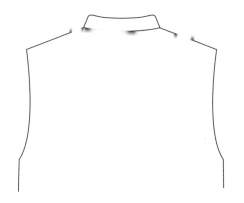

COLLARS

FRONT VIEWS

PETER PAN COLLAR

BACK VIEWS

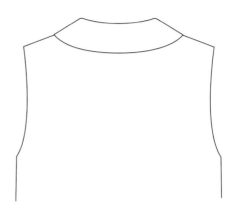

ETON COLLAR

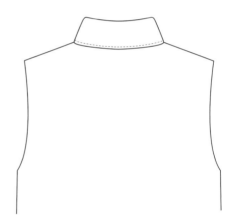

SAILOR COLLAR

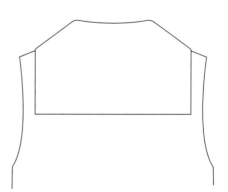

VARIATIONS

FRONT VIEWS
BERTHA COLLAR

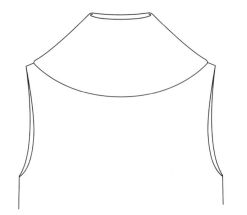

BOW-TIED/PUSSY BOW

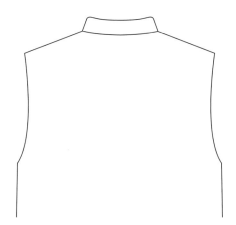

CASCADE/JABOT

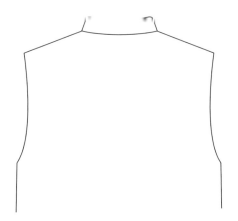

COLLARS

PURITAN/PILGRIM COLLAR

BACK VIEWS

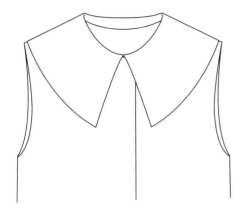

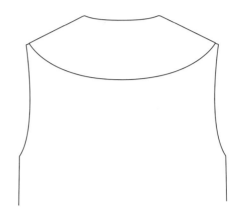

PIERROT COLLAR

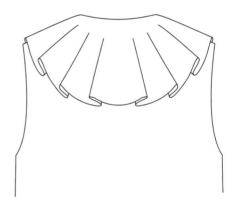

POLO COLLAR

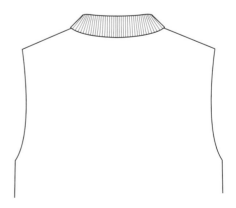

KEY BASIC SHAPES

SET-IN SLEEVE
FRONT VIEW

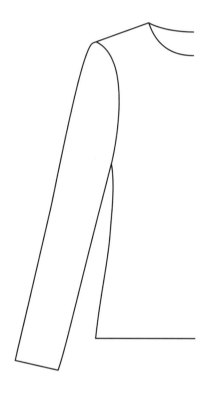

BACK VIEW

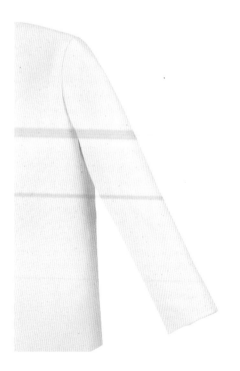

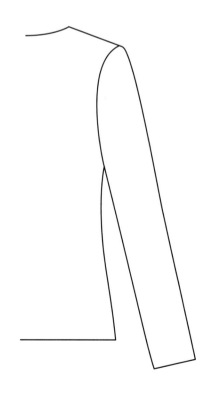

SLEEVES

DROPPED SLEEVE/DROPPED SHOULDER
FRONT VIEW

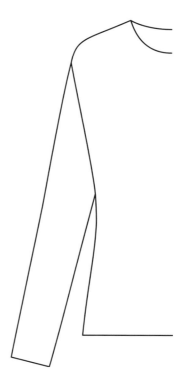

BACK VIEW

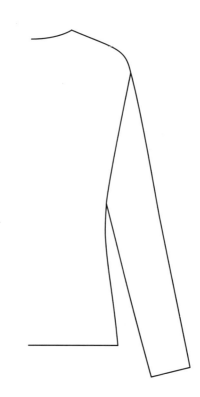

KEY BASIC SHAPES

ONE-PIECE SLEEVE
FRONT VIEW

 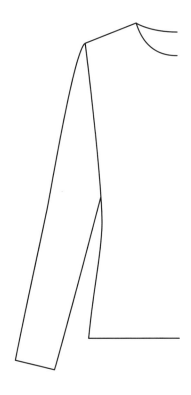

BACK VIEW

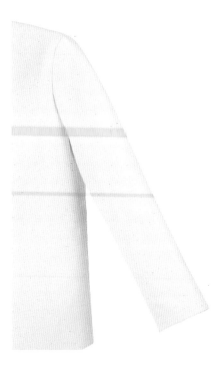 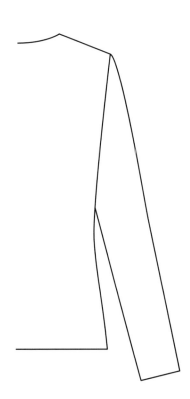

SLEEVES

TWO-PIECE SLEEVE
FRONT VIEW

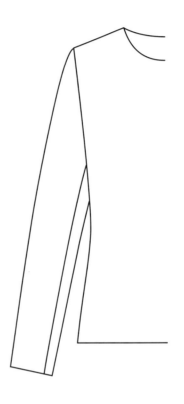

BACK VIEW

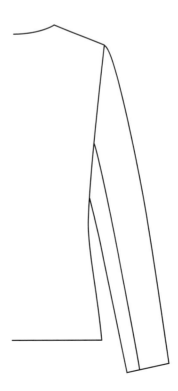

KEY BASIC SHAPES

FITTED SLEEVE
FRONT VIEW

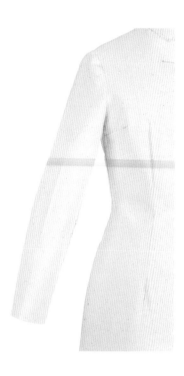

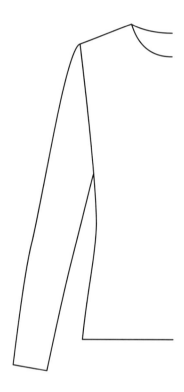

BACK VIEW

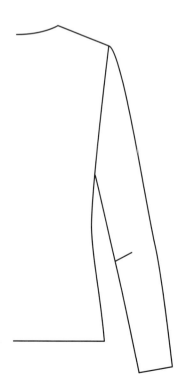

SLEEVES

SHIRT SLEEVE
FRONT VIEW

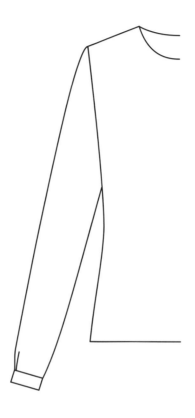

BACK VIEW

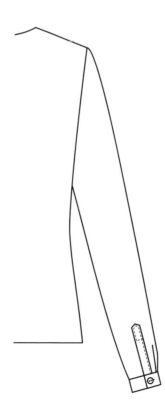

VARIATIONS

FRONT VIEWS
CAP SLEEVE

PUFF SLEEVE

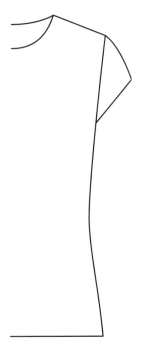

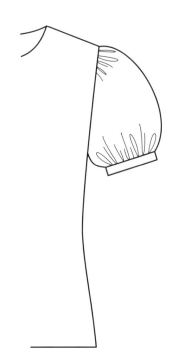

BACK VIEWS

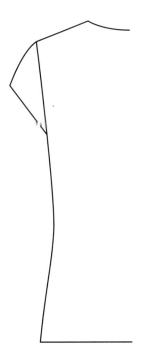

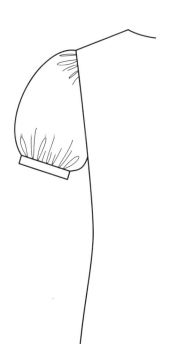

SLEEVES

FRONT VIEWS
BELL SLEEVE

CAPE/FLARED/BUTTERFLY SLEEVE

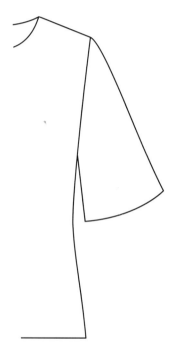

BACK VIEWS

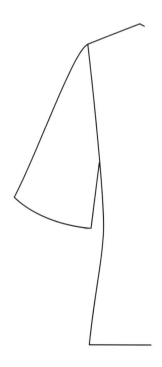

VARIATIONS

FRONT VIEWS
LANTERN SLEEVE

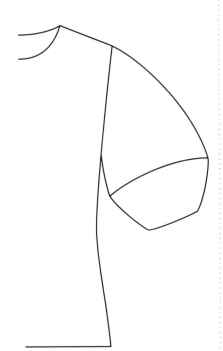

PAGODA SLEEVE

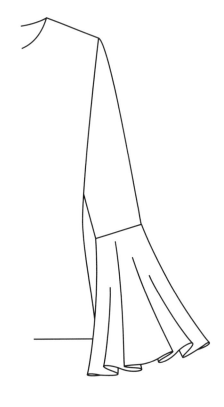

PEASANT SLEEVE

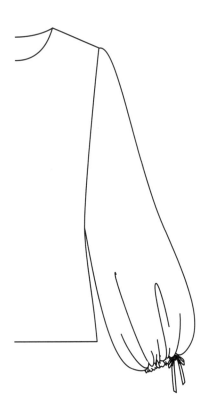

BACK VIEWS

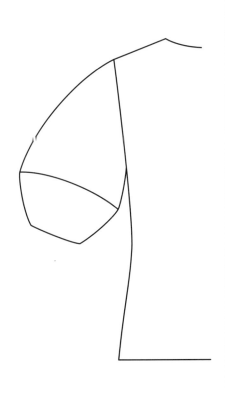

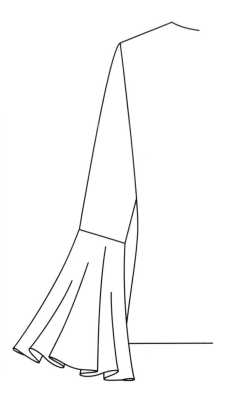

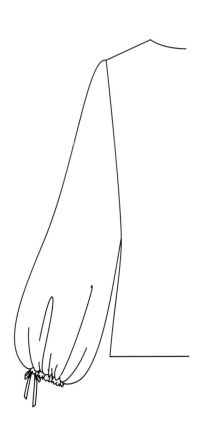

SLEEVES

FRONT VIEWS
KIMONO SLEEVE

RAGLAN SLEEVE

BACK VIEWS

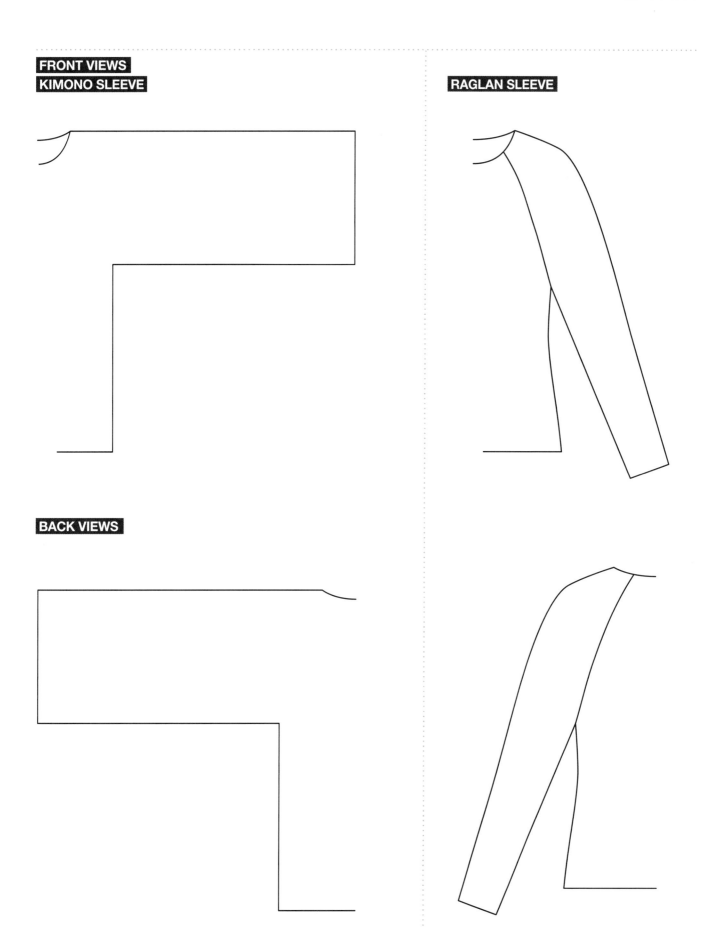

VARIATIONS

FRONT VIEWS
DOLMAN/MAGYAR SLEEVE/BATWING

KITE SLEEVE

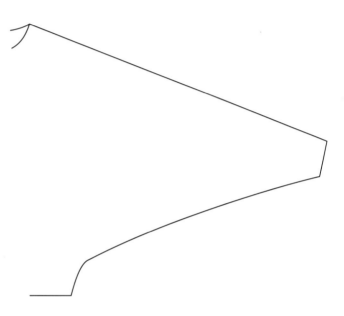

BACK VIEWS

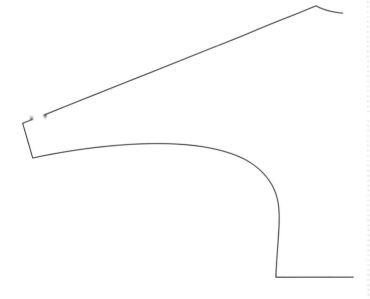

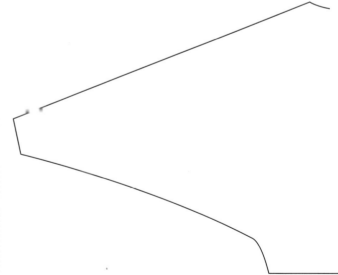

SLEEVES

FRONT VIEWS

BISHOP SLEEVE

LEG-OF-MUTTON SLEEVE

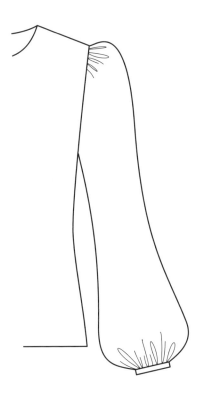

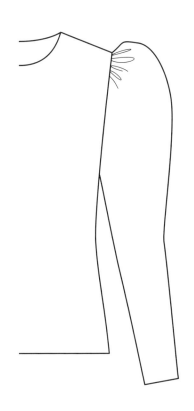

BACK VIEWS

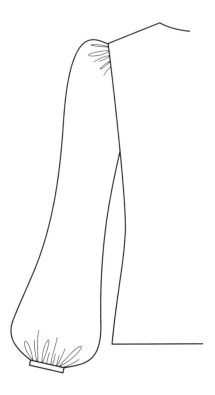

KEY BASIC SHAPES

. . . .

SINGLE/BARREL CUFF WITH PLACKET
FRONT VIEW

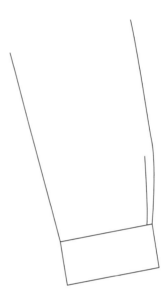

BACK VIEW

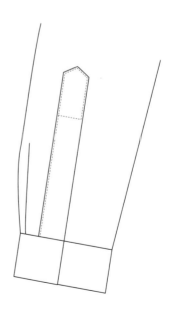

CUFFS

FRENCH CUFF
FRONT VIEW

 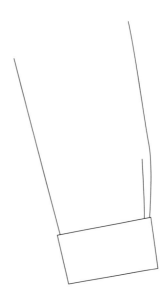

BACK VIEW

 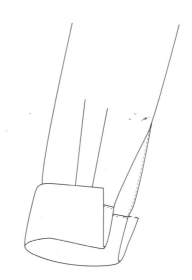

KEY BASIC SHAPES

. . . .

BOUND CUFF
FRONT VIEW

 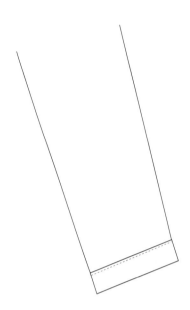

BACK VIEW

 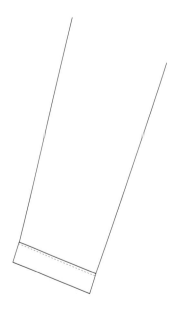

CUFFS

DRAWSTRING CUFF
FRONT VIEW

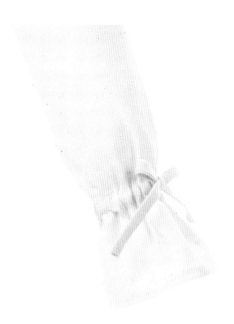 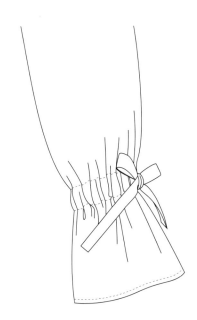

BACK VIEW

 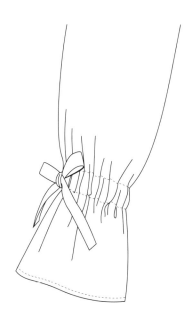

POCKETS

PATCH POCKET

FLAP POCKET

WELT/JETTED/PIPED/BESOM POCKET

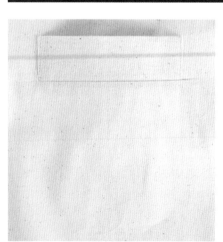 

DETAILS

BELLOWS/CARGO/SAFARI POCKET

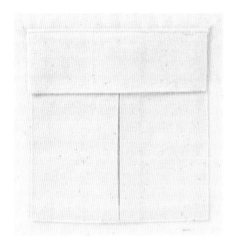 

IN-A-SEAM POCKET (EXTERNAL VIEW)

 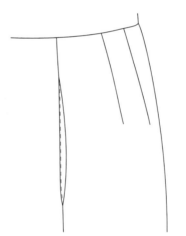

IN-A-SEAM POCKET (INTERNAL VIEW)

CONSTRUCTION DETAILS

DART

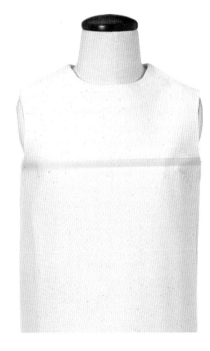

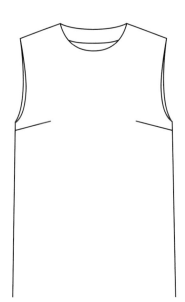

TUCK

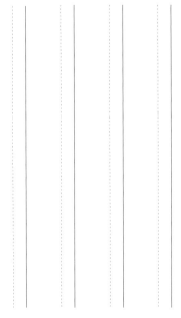

DETAILS

GATHERS

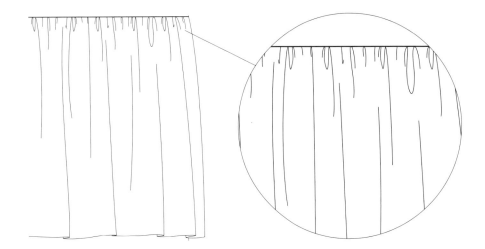

GUSSET

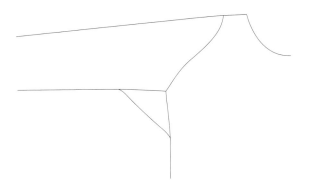

YOKE
FRONT VIEW

BACK VIEW

CONSTRUCTION DETAILS

BINDING

MITRE
FRONT VIEW

BACK VIEW

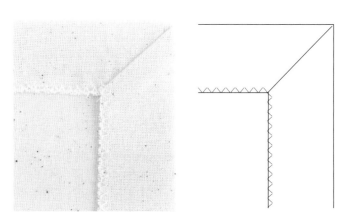

ROLLED HEM

DETAILS

INSEAM
FRONT VIEW

BACK VIEW

FRAYED EDGE

DESIGN DETAILS

PIPING

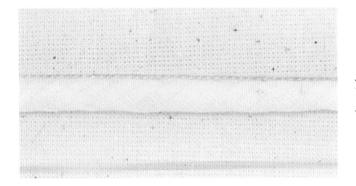

RUFFLE/FRILL

 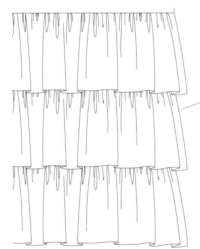 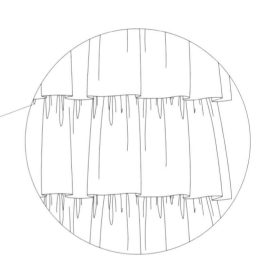

TAB CUFF

 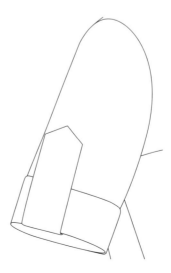

DETAILS

PLACKET

 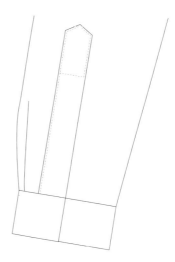

CONCEALED PLACKET

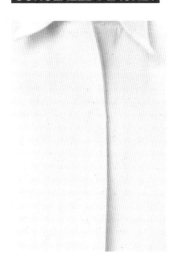 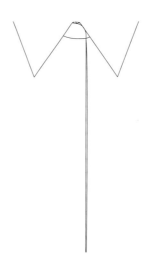

BELT LOOP

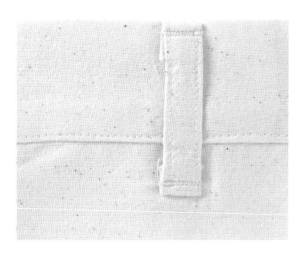 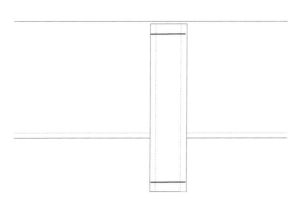

DESIGN DETAILS

COLLAR STAND

FRONT VIEW

BACK VIEW

ZIPPED FLY

UNZIPPED

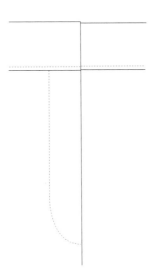

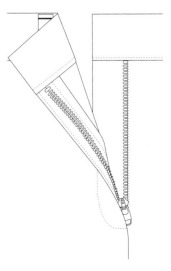

GODET

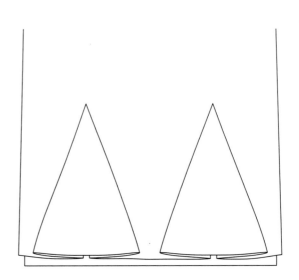

DETAILS

VENT

 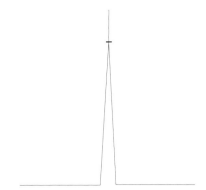

EPAULET

 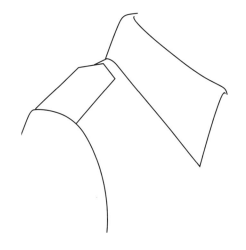

RIB (1)

 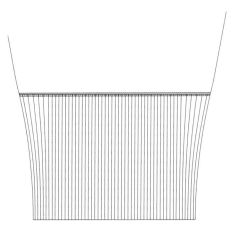

DESIGN DETAILS

RIB (2)

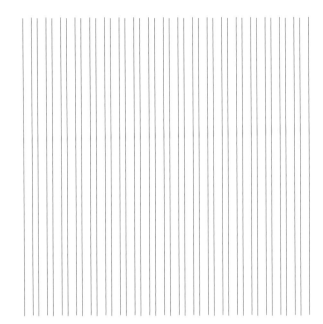

RIB (3)

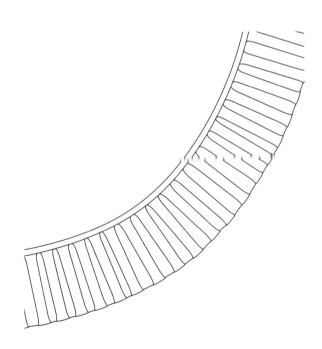

DETAILS

TURN UP

 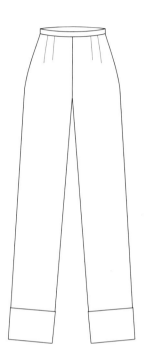

HOOD

 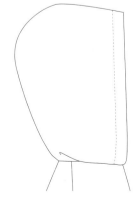

DECORATIVE DESIGN DETAILS

RUCHING

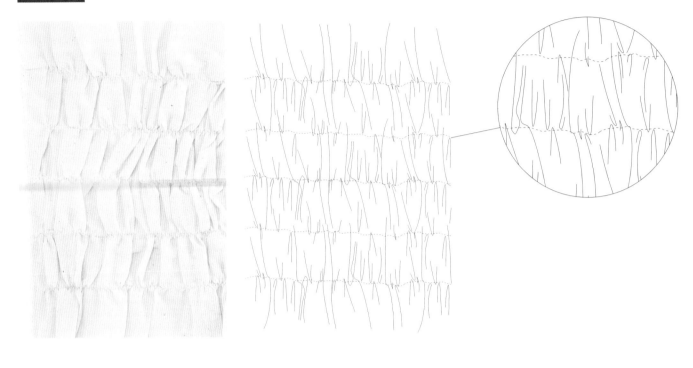

SMOCKING

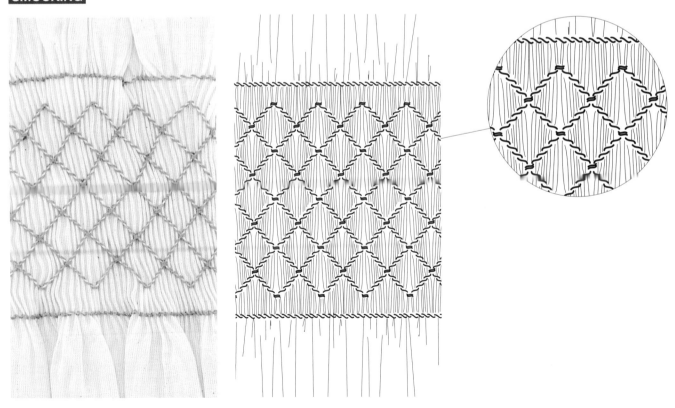

DETAILS

SCALLOP

 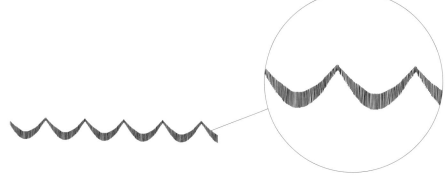

SHIRRING

 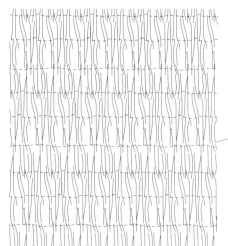 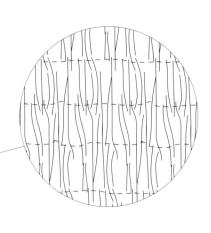

QUILTING

  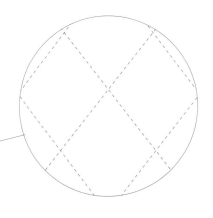

DECORATIVE DESIGN DETAILS

APPLIQUE

TASSEL

FRINGE

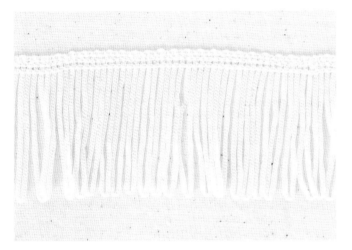 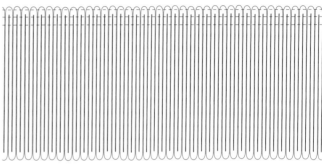

POM POM

 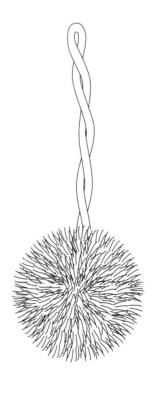

PLEATS

ACCORDION PLEAT

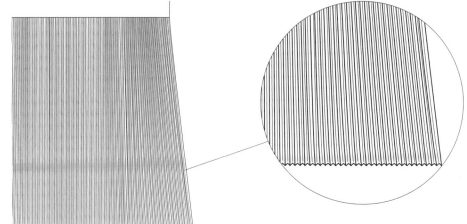

KNIFE PLEAT

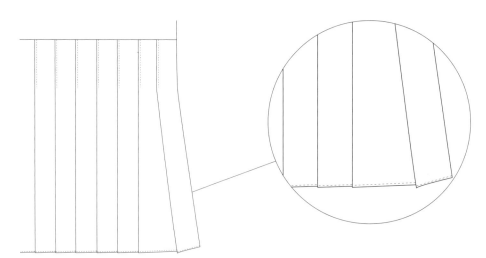

BOX PLEAT

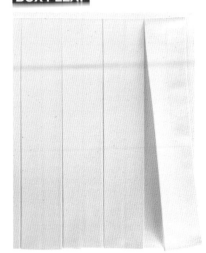
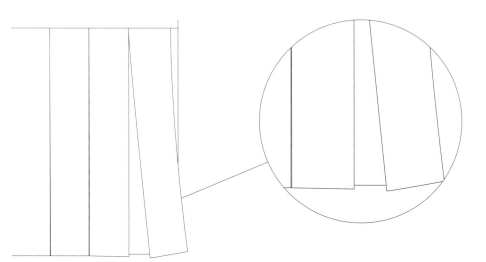

DETAILS

PLEATS

INVERTED PLEAT

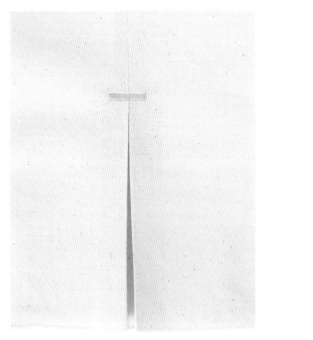 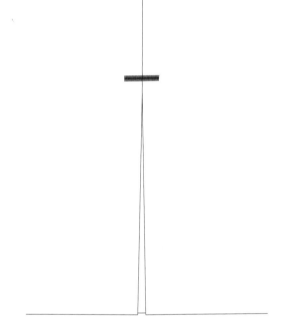

KICK PLEAT

SEAMS

TOP STITCH/RUNNING STITCH (SINGLE ROW)

TOP STITCH/RUNNING STITCH (DOUBLE ROW)

FLAT FELL/TWIN NEEDLE

FRENCH SEAM

SEAMS

BOUND SEAM

EDGE STITCH

LAPPED SEAM

CHANNEL/SLOT SEAM

STITCHES

STRAIGHT LOCKSTITCH

TWIN NEEDLE

ZIG ZAG

DETAILS

OVERLOCKING

BLIND STITCH/HEM STITCH

BLANKET STITCH

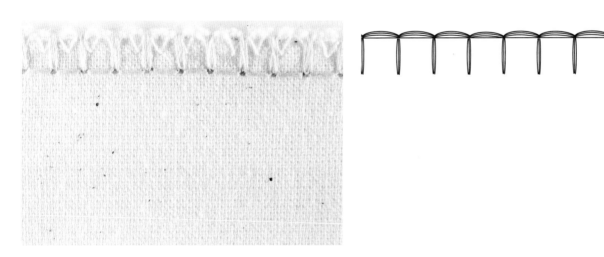

STITCHES

CROSS STITCH

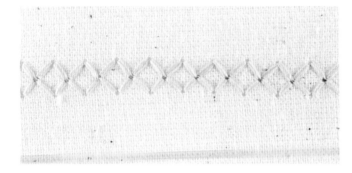 

CHAIN STITCH

BAR TACK

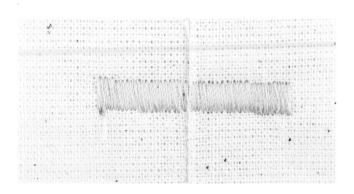 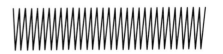

FASTENINGS/HARDWARE

FOUR-HOLE BUTTON

 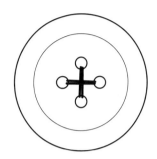

TWO-HOLE BUTTON

 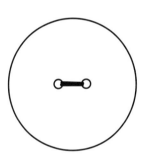

COVERED BUTTON

 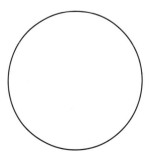

FASTENINGS / HARDWARE

POPPER/PRESS STUD/SNAP

HOOK & EYE (UNDONE)

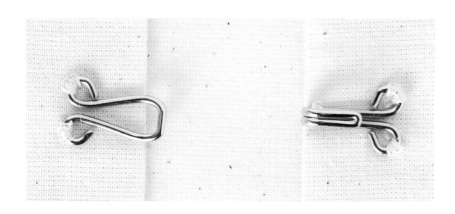 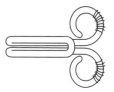

HOOK & EYE (DONE UP)

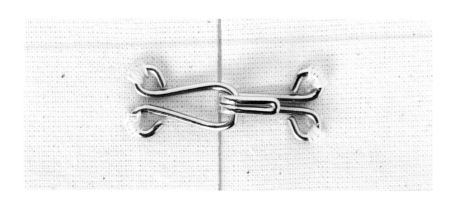 

DETAILS

FASTENINGS / HARDWARE

TIE (UNTIED)

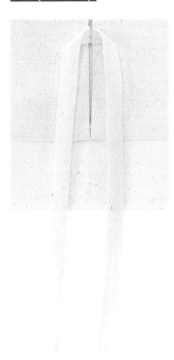 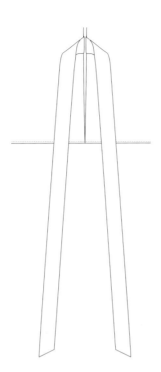

TIE (TIED IN A BOW)

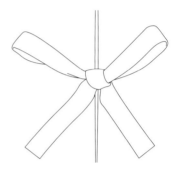

CHINESE KNOT

TOGGLE

FASTENINGS / HARDWARE

FROGS/FROGGING

ROULEAU/BUTTON AND LOOP

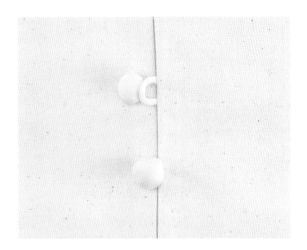 

MACHINED BUTTONHOLE

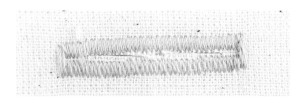 

DETAILS

FASTENINGS / HARDWARE

KEYHOLE

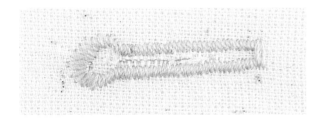 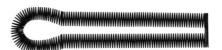

BOUND BUTTONHOLE

 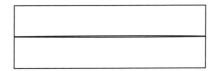

INVISIBLE ZIP

 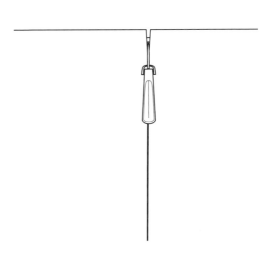

FASTENINGS / HARDWARE

VISIBLE ZIP

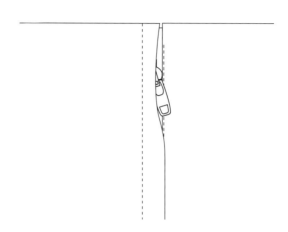

TWO-WAY ZIP

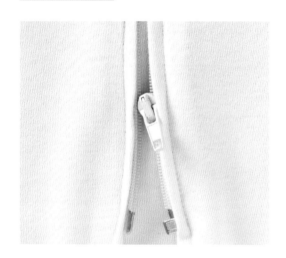

VELCRO

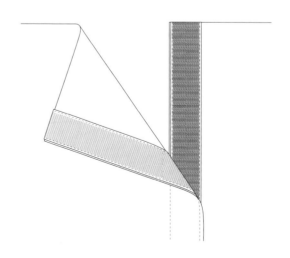

DETAILS

FASTENINGS / HARDWARE

EYELETS/GROMMETS

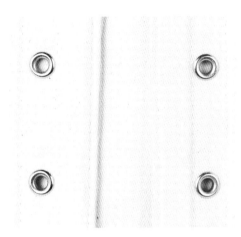 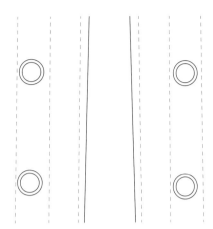

LACING

 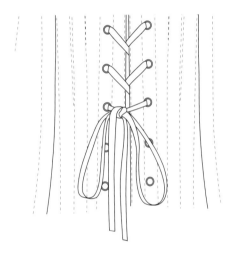

STUD

 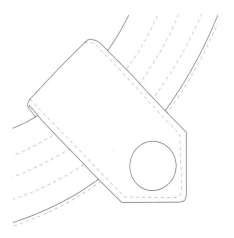

FASTENINGS / HARDWARE

RIVET

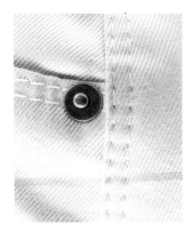 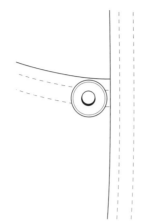

DRAWSTRING TOGGLE

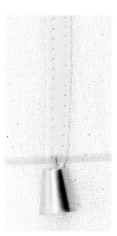

D-RING

 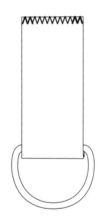

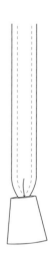

BUCKLE

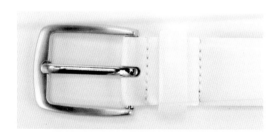 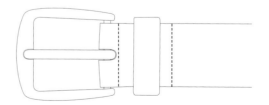

GLOSSARY, INDEX AND RESOURCES

GLOSSARY

A
A-line Garment that flares out from shoulder or waist to hem, like the letter 'A'.
Apparel Generic term for clothing.
Asymmetric Garments or details that are different on the right-hand side than the left.

C
CAD Computer-aided design.
Centre-line Vertical line drawn down the middle of a sheet of paper as the starting point for a technical drawing template.
Collar Stand Band of material attached to the neckline of a garment to support the collar.
Colouring-up Rendering a drawing to show colour, texture or pattern.
Colourway One of a range of colours or colour combinations used to create a garment.
Costing Sheet List of all the elements needed to make up a garment (fabric, trims, cost of manufacture), which is then used to calculate the manufacturing, gross margin and selling price of a style.

D
Dart Tapered tuck stitched into a garment in order to fit it to the body.
Double-breasted Garment, usually a coat or jacket, with a wide overlap at the font, wrapping over the breast and fastening with buttons. Two rows of button are visible when closed.

F
Flats Chiefly US term for technical drawings.
Frogging Braided or corded decorative fastening.

G
Godet Triangular piece of fabric inserted into a garment to add fullness.
Gusset Triangular or diamond-shaped piece of fabric inserted into a garment to reinforce or expand part of it. Generally used under the arm or at the crotch.

H
Hardware The – traditionally metal – closures, fixings and decorative additions on a garment.

L
Lapel One of two triangular flaps below the collar, pressed back to the chest, on jackets, coats and shirts.
Light Box Table-top box, usually made from acrylic, that is illuminated from the rear, assisting with tracing and design work.
Line Sheet Sales document presenting information such as style, colours, fabrics, order quantities, delivery period, manufacturing and selling prices along with garment sketches to wholesale buyers. Also called a range sheet.
Look Book Designers' or manufacturers' portfolio presenting a season's range; can include technical drawings, catwalk shots and illustrations.

M
Mannequin Dummy of the human body used to display clothing.

Merchandising Plan Graphic representation of a store floor area in 2D or 3D used to plan the display of garments prior to the collection arriving in store.

O
Outerwear Garments designed to be worn over the top of other items of clothing.

P
Placket Opening in a garment that allows the wearer to put it on. Usually positioned at the waist, collar, cuffs and neck of a garment.
Plan View Head-on perspective view of a garment.
Plus Size Clothing made especially for larger figures that go beyond the traditional range of sizes.
Princess Line Garment, usually a women's coat, which is fitted at the waist and flares out towards the hem.

R
Range Board Presentation of a collection of co-ordinating garment styles showing individual styles and colourways.
Range Sheet Sales document presenting information such as style, colours, fabrics, order quantities, delivery period, manufacturing and selling prices along with garment sketches to wholesale buyers. Also called a line sheet.
Rever Wide lapel that is turned back to show the reverse side.
Rivet Type of metal fastener used in garment construction.

S
Set-in Refers to part of a garment that has been inserted, eg a sleeve that has been sewn into an armhole rather than cut as part of the bodice.
Sketch Rough, spontaneous drawing of a garment idea that is not necessarily accurate or in proportion.
Specification Sheet (or 'spec') Includes a technical drawing (including front and back views and, if necessary, a side view and internal views), plus all detailed measurements required to produce the garment.
Speed Designing A shortcut to producing technical drawings. Once a garment style has been drawn using the generic template, that style can then be used as a template for developing any number of variations. Facilitates the drawing of real working garments, rather than just sketching out rough ideas.

T
Technical Drawing Also known as 'flats', 'working drawings' or 'line drawings', technical drawings are an accurate representation of a garment.
Toile Trial garment created during the early design stages so the garment can be seen three-dimensionally and fit and drape assessed. Usually made in calico cotton or a cloth that replicates the final intended fabric.
Trend Books Industry publications that can contain mood photographs, fabric swatches and technical drawings, intended to provide a forecast

of new ideas for future seasons.

V
Vent An opening in a garment to allow for ventilation or ease of movement.

W
Welt Border used to decorate or reinforce part of a garment, such as a pocket or seam.

Y
Yoke A fitted piece of fabric, usually across the shoulders (in shirts, coats, etc) or hips (in skirts and trousers), to which the rest of the garment is attached.

USEFUL PROFESSIONAL ASSOCIATIONS

EUROPE

UK

British Apparel and Textile Confederation (BATC)
5 Portland Place, London W1N 3AA
Tel: +44 (0)20 7636 7788
Fax: +44 (0)20 7636 7515
Email: batc@dial.pipex.com
Website: www.apparel-textiles.co.uk

British Clothing Industry Association (BCIA)
5 Portland Place, London W1B 1PW
Tel: +44 (0)20 7636 7788 or +44 (0)20 7636 5577
Fax: +44 (0)20 7636 7515
Email: contact@5portlandplace.org.uk
Website: www.5portlandplace.org.uk

British Fashion Council (BFC)
5 Portland Place, London W1B 1PW
Tel: + 44 (0)20 7636 7788
Fax: +44 (0)20 7436 5924
Email: emmacampbell@britishfashioncouncil.com
www.britishfashioncouncil.com

EMTEX LTD (Designer Forum)
69–73 Lower Parliament Street,
    Nottingham NG1 3BB
Tel: +44 (0)115 9115339
Fax: +44 (0)115 911 5345
Email: info@design-online.net
Website: www.design-online.net

Fashion and Design Protection Association Ltd.
69 Lawrence Road, London N15 4EY
Tel: +44 (0)20 8800 5777
Fax: +44 (0)20 8880 2882
Email: info@fdpa.co.uk
Website: www.fdpa.co.uk

Northern Ireland Textile and Apparel Assoc. Ltd.
5c The Square, Hillsborough BT26 6AG
Tel: +44 (0)2892 68 9999
Fax: +44 (0)2892 68 9968
Email: info@nita.co.uk

Register of Apparel & Textile Designers
5 Portland Place, London W1N 3AA
Tel: +44 (0)20 7636 5577
Fax: +44 (0)20 7436 5924
Email: contact@5portlandplace.org.uk
Website: www.5portlandplace.org.uk

France

Chambres Syndicale de la Couture Parisienne
45 Rue Saint-Roch, 75001 Paris
Tel: + 33 (0)1 4261 0077
Fax: +33 (0)1 4286 8942
Email: ecole@modeaparis.com
Website: www.modeaparis.com

Fédération Francais du Prét-à-Porter Féminine
5 Rue Caumartin, 75009 Paris
Tel: +33 (0)1 4494 7030
Fax: +33 (0)1 4494 7004
Email: contact@pretparis.com
Website: www.pretaporter.com

Fédération Française des Industries du
    Vêtement Masculin
8 Rue Montesquieu, 75001 Paris
Tel. : +33 (0)1 44 55 66 50
Fax : +33 (0)1 44 55 66 65
Website: www.lamodefrancaise.org.fr

Germany

Confederation of the German Textile
    and Fashion Industry
Frankfurter Strasse 10–14, D-65760 Eschborn
Tel: +49 6196 9660
Fax: +49 6196 42170
Email: info@textil-mode.de
Website: www.textil-mode.de

Italy

Associazione Italiana della Filiera Tessile
    Abbigliamento SMI
Federazione Tessile e Moda
Viale Sarca 223, 20126 Milano
Tel: +39 (0)2-641191
Fax: +39 (0)2-66103667 / 70
Website: www.smi-ati.it
Email: info@sistemamodaitalia.it

Centro di Firenze per la Moda Italiana
Via Faenzan, 111, 50123, Florence
Tel: +39 (0)553 6931
Fax: +39 (0)5536 93200
Email: cfmi@cfmi.it
Website: www.cfmi.it

Spain

Association of New and Young Spanish Designers
Segovia 22, Bajos CP 28005 Madrid
Tel: +34 915 475 857
Fax: +34 915 475 857
Email: nuevosdisenadores@telefonica.net

ASIA AND THE PACIFIC

Australia

Council of Textiles and Fashion Industries,
    Australia Ltd (TFIA)
Level 2, 20 Queens Road, Melbourne, VIC 3004
Tel: +61 (0) 38317 6666
Fax: +61 (0) 38317 6666
Email: info@tfia.com.au
Website: www.tfia.com.au

Design Institute of Australia
486 Albert Street, East Melbourne, VIC 3002,
    GPO Box 4352
Tel: +61 (0) 38662 5490
Fax: +61 (0) 38662 5358
Email: admin@design.org.au
Website: www.dia.org.au

Australian Fashion Council
Showroom 16, 23–25 Gipps Street,
    Collingwood VIC 3066
Tel: +61 (0) 38680 9400
Fax: +61 (0) 38680 9499
Email: info@australianfashioncouncil.com
Website: www.australianfashioncouncil.com

Melbourne Design and Fashion Incubator (MDFI)
Shop 238, Level 2, Central Shopping Centre, 211
    La Trobe Street, Melbourne 3000, Victoria
Tel: +61 (0) 39671 4522
Email: info@fashionincubator.com.au
Website: www.fashionincubator.com.au

China

China National Textile and Apparel Council
China Textile Network Company, Rm 236, No 12,
    Dong Chang'an Street, Beijing 100740
Tel: +86 10 85229 100

Fax: +86 10 85229 100
Email: einfo@ml.ctei.gov.cn
Website: www.ctei.gov.cn

China Fashion Designers Association
Room 154, No 12, Dong Chang'an Street,
    Beijing, 100742
Tel: +86 1085 229427
Fax: +86 1085 229037

Japan

Japan Fashion Association
Fukushima Building, 1-5-3 Nihonbashi –
    Muromachi, Chuo – ku, Tokyo 103-0022
Tel: +81 33242 1677
Fax: +81 33242 1678
Email: info@japanfashion.or.jp
Website: japanfashion.or.jp

Japan Association of Specialist in Textile
    and Apparel
Jasta Office, 2-11-13-205, Shiba – koen,
    Minato – Ku, Tokyo 105-0011
Tel: +81 03 3437 6416
Fax: +81 03 3437 3194
Email: jasta@mtb.biglobe.ne.jp
Website: jasta1.or.jp/index_english.html

NORTH AMERICA

USA

American Apparel and Footwear Association
1601 N Kent Street, Suite 1200, Arlington VA
    22209
Tel: +1 703 524 1864
Fax: +1 703 522 6741
Website: www.apparelandfootwear.org

Council of Fashion Designers of America
1412 Broadway Suite 2006, New York, NY 10018
Tel: +1 212 302 1821
Website: www.cfda.com

Fashion Group International New York
8 West 40th Street, 7th Floor, New York,
    NY 10018
Tel: +1 212 302 5511
Fax: +1 212 302 5533
Email: e-cheryl@fgi.org
Website: www.fgi.org

International Textile and Apparel Association
ITAA 6060 Sunrise Vista Drive, Suite 1300,
    Citrus Heights, CA 95610
Tel: +1 916 723 1628
Email: info@itaaonline.org
Website: www.itaaonline.org

Brazilian–American Fashion Association
    (BRAMFSA)
PO Box 83-2036, Delray Beach, Florida 33483
Email: bramfsa@bramfsa.com

Canada

Canadian Apparel Federation
124 O'Connor Street, Suite 504, Ottawa, Ontario
    K1P 5M9
Tel: +1 613 231 3220
Fax: +1 613 231 2305
Email: info@apparel.ca
Website: www.apparel.ca

INDEX

FURTHER READING

Abling, Bina and Kathleen Maggio, *Integrating Draping, Drafting and Drawing,* Fairchild, 2008

Centner, Marianne, and Frances Vereker, *Adobe Illustrator: A Fashion Designer's Handbook,* Blackwell, 2007

Aldrich, Winifred, *Metric Pattern Cutting for Children's Wear and Babywear,* Blackwell Publishing, 4th edition, 2009

Aldrich, Winifred, *Metric Pattern Cutting for Menswear, Blackwell Publishing,* 4th edition, 2008

Aldrich, Winifred, *Metric Pattern Cutting for Womenswear,* Blackwell Publishing, 5th edition, 2008

Armstrong, Helen Joseph, *Patternmaking for Fashion Design,* Pearson Education, 4th edition, 2005

Bray, Natalie, *Dress Pattern Designing,* Blackwell Publishing, 2003

Burke, Sandra, *Fashion Artist: Drawing Techniques to Portfolio Presentation,* Burke Publishing, 2nd edition, 2006

Burke, Sandra, *Fashion Computing - Design Techniques and CAD,* Burke Publishing, 2006

Campbell, Hilary, *Designing Patterns - A Fresh Approach to Pattern Cutting,* Nelson Thornes, 1980

Cooklin, Gerry, *Garment Technology for Fashion Designers,* Blackwell, 1997

Cooklin, Gerry, *Pattern Cutting for Women's Outerwear,* OM Books, 2008

Fischer, Annette, *Basics Fashion Design: Construction,* AVA Publishing SA, 2009

Ireland, Patrick John, *New Encyclopedia Of Fashion Details,* B T Batsford Ltd, 2008

Knowles, Lori A, *The Practical Guide To Patternmaking For Fashion Designers: Menswear,* Fairchild, 2005

Knowles, Lori A, *The Practical Guide To Patternmaking For Fashion Designers: Juniors, Misses, And Women,* Fairchild, 2005

Lazear, Susan, *Adobe Illustrator for Fashion Design,* Prentice Hall, 2008

Lazear, Susan, *Adobe Photoshop for Fashion Design,* Prentice Hall, 2009

McKelvey, Kathryn, *Fashion Source Book,* Blackwell; 2nd Edition, 2006

Peacock, John, *The Complete Fashion Sourcebook: 2,000 Illustrations Charting 20th-Century Fashion,* Thames & Hudson, 2005

Riegelman, Nancy, *9 Heads: A Guide to Drawing Fashion,* Prentice Hall, 3rd edition, 2006

Rosen, Sylvia, *Patternmaking: A Comprehensive Reference for Fashion Design,* Prentice Hall, 2004

Seivewright, Simon, *Basics Fashion Design: Research and Design,* AVA Publishing SA, 2007

Stipelman, Steven, *Illustrating Fashion: Concept To Creation,* Fairchild, 2nd edition, 2005

Tallon, Kevin, *Creative Computer Fashion Design with Illustrator,* 2006

Travers-Spencer, Simon, and Zarida Zaman, *The Fashion Designer's Directory of Shape and Style,* Barron's Educational Series, 2008

Ward, Janet, *Pattern Cutting and Making Up: The Professional Approach,* 2nd edition, Butterworth-Heinemann, 1987

PHOTO CREDITS

The authors and publisher would like to thank the following institutions and individuals who provided images for use in this book. In all cases, every effort has been made to credit the copyright holders, but should there be any omissions or errors the publisher would be pleased to insert the appropriate acknowledgment in any subsequent edition of this book.

p11 Ayako Koyama
p12 Wayne Fitzel
p13 (top) Wayne Fitzell; (bottom) Debenhams
p14 Look Book images, Patrick Lee Yow
p15 Toby Meadows
p16 Worth Global Style Network
p17 (top) Senso Group; (bottom) Ayako Koyama
p18 & 19 Vogue Patterns, courtesy of McCall, Butterick & Vogue
p20-23 Ayako Koyama
p26-31 Photography by PSC Photography Ltd.
p32-35 Tutorials by Ayako Koyama
p36-39 Ayako Koyama
p50 (left) Vanda Rulewska; (right) Patrick Lee Yow)
p51 (top) Mary Ruppert; (middle) Lynn Blake; (bottom) Maritza Cantero-Farrell

All technical drawings in section two by Ayako Koyama; all toile photography by Packshot.com

AUTHOR'S ACKNOWLEDGMENTS

I would like to especially thank Ayako Koyama for creating all of the technical drawings for the directory, and Anne Stafford and Ayako for creating all the beautiful toiles. Thanks to you both for your focus, dedication and patience with me! An important thank you to Eleanor Warrington for introducing me to the world of 'flats' and commercial design so many years ago, in my first ever internship while still at college: that's when fashion design was demystified for me, when I came to understand commercial design, and when it all started....
Basia would also like to thank the following individuals and organizations:

Jo Lightfoot
Anne Townley
Gaynor Sermon
Melanie Mues
Patrick Lee Yow
Wayne Fitzell
Vanda Rulewska
Sarah Bailey
Melanie Cunningham
Toby Meadows
Sean Chiles
Kathryn Kujawa
Bridget Miles
Mary Ruppert-Stroescu
Lynn Blake
Maritza Cantero-Farrell
Keith Jones at McCall, Butterick & Vogue Patterns (www.butterick-vogue.co.uk)
WGSN (Worth Global Style Network)
Kane Thompson and Ann-Louise Tingelof at Senso Group, (www.Sensogroup.co.uk)

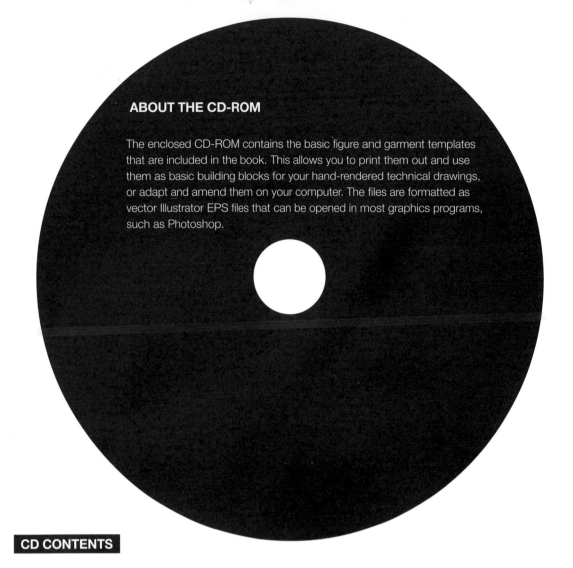

ABOUT THE CD-ROM

The enclosed CD-ROM contains the basic figure and garment templates that are included in the book. This allows you to print them out and use them as basic building blocks for your hand-rendered technical drawings, or adapt and amend them on your computer. The files are formatted as vector Illustrator EPS files that can be opened in most graphics programs, such as Photoshop.

CD CONTENTS